ANCIENT PLACES

ANCIENT PLACES

PEOPLE AND LANDSCAPE
in the EMERGING NORTHWEST

JACK NISBET

Illustrations by Hannah Small

SASQUATCH BOOKS
SEATTLE

For Claire

In memory of Ann, Merle, and John

Printed in the United States of America

Published by Sasquatch Books
19 18 17 16 15   9 8 7 6 5 4 3 2 1

Editor: Gary Luke
Production editor: Em Gale
Cover illustration: "Aspen Camp 27 Miles from Cow Creek," James Madison Alden, 1860; Alden Sketch #17, Entry 221, Record Group 76; National Archives at College Park, College Park, MD.
Design: Joyce Hwang
Illustrations: Hannah Small
Copyeditor: Elizabeth Johnson

Library of Congress Cataloging-in-Publication Data is available.

ISBN: 978-1-57061-980-9

Sasquatch Books
1904 Third Avenue, Suite 710
Seattle, WA 98101
(206) 467-4300
www.sasquatchbooks.com
custserv@sasquatchbooks.com

Portions of some of these essays have appeared in *Cascadia Chronicle*, the *North Columbia Monthly*, the *Inlander*, *We Proceeded On*, and HistoryLink.org.

Contents

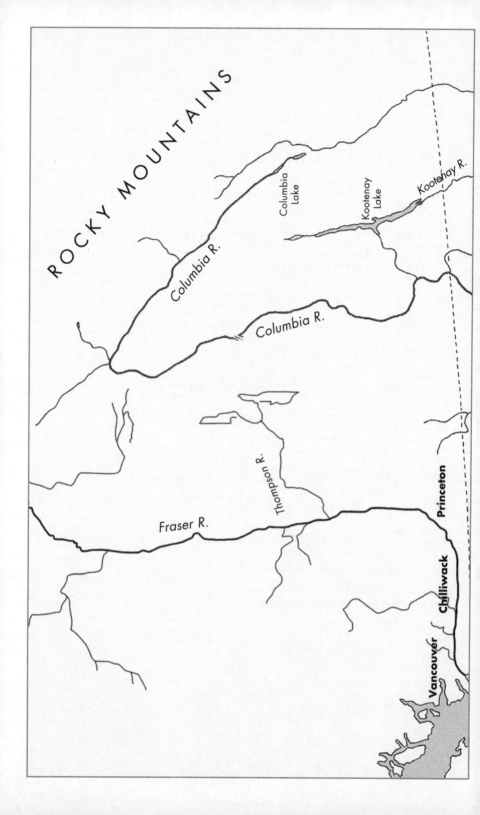

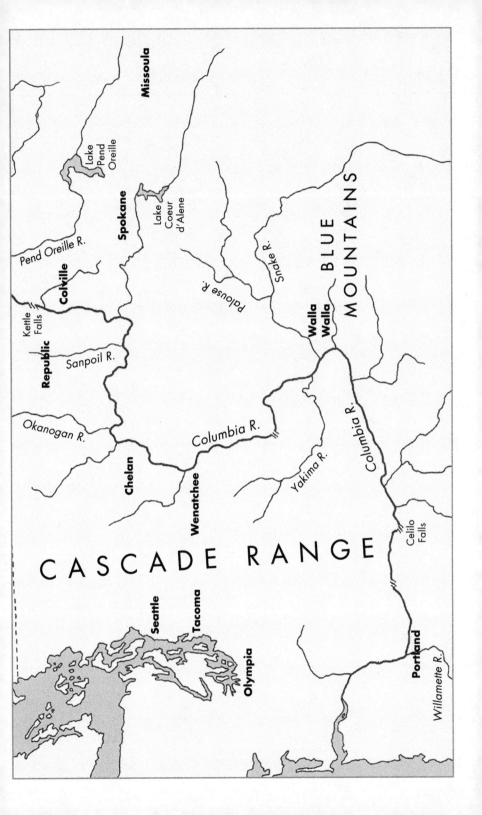

I

CHASING THE ELECTRIC FLUID

Innumerable Luminous Pieces

In early November 1792, Hudson's Bay Company fur agent David Thompson led a crew of hungry men through the wilderness of lakes that extended north and west of their York Factory headquarters on the bay. They had found the fishing and hunting very poor around their isolated trade house and had fanned out in hopes of better luck. Thompson and a lanky Scottish lad named Andrew Davy tried Lake Susquagemow (now called Landing Lake in modern Manitoba)—a sizeable sheet of water around thirty miles long and four or five miles wide. Since the lake's ice was not yet thick enough for secure walking, the pair roamed its edges in search of grouse and hare. After some time, they came upon a frozen marsh, where they spotted a beaver lodge surrounded by a small pool of open water, which the animals kept ice-free by swimming around it in the evening.

By the time November's early dusk fell, Thompson and Davy, muskets in hand, had settled into watchful positions near the domed lodge. After a full moon rose over the east end of the lake, a solitary beaver emerged from one of the entry tunnels. Davy eased his firearm into position and pulled the trigger. The musket misfired with a loud snap; the beaver slapped the water with its tail "as if to bid us good night," wrote Thompson, "and plunged into his house."

That slap ended any hope of a successful hunt. Yet the evening was pleasant, and the pair continued to loiter beside the marsh until nearly eleven o'clock. They were about to call it a night when a brilliant light, rivaling the recent moonrise, appeared over the east end of the lake. "It was a Meteor of globular form, and appeared larger than the Moon."

The "meteor"—in Thompson's day, the term could apply to any visual atmospheric event, from hailstones to a lightning flash—seemed to travel directly down the length of the lake toward them, descending through the air as it approached. "When within three hundred yards of us, it struck the River ice with a sound like a mass of jelly," Thompson wrote. Then it "dashed into innumerable luminous pieces, and instantly expired. Andrew would have run away but he had no time to do so; curiosity chained me to the spot."

Next morning, true to his curious nature, Thompson returned to the beaver marsh to look for evidence of the crash. He was astonished to find none whatsoever, even though the snow clearly showed his lightest footprints from the night before. He had read accounts of fiery meteorites in Europe that exploded with a loud noise or threw off a fusillade of stones, but the only sound he could recall from this event was the flop of tossed jelly.

Thompson had arrived at Hudson Bay almost a decade earlier, as a young teenager, and he had traveled extensively throughout the north country. On more than one occasion, when journeying along an expanse of water, he had observed "phenomena that are peculiar to such a surface." He had noticed that during the early part of each winter, clear and calm nights gave rise to "innumerable very small luminous, meteoric points, which are visible for the twinkling of an eye, and disappear." When these momentary sparkles gained intensity, he found, the wind was bound to rise.

Several days later, the fur agent was back near the same marsh on Lake Susquagemow, hunting for game in an open grove of aspen trees. About six in the evening, another concentrated light from the lake's east end lit up the premoon darkness. Thompson thought that this "meteor" appeared larger than the first one he had seen, but not as bright, and he tried to track it carefully. The glowing globe dove right into the aspen grove, at a height of about eight feet above the ground. "As it struck the trees, pieces flew from it, and went out . . . it passed close by me striking the trees with the sound of a mass of jelly . . . although it must have lost much of its size from the many trees it struck, it went out of my sight, [still] a large mass."

Searching for answers about the nature of these strange gelatinous lights, Thompson went out the next day and examined the trees that had been struck, only to find that they were completely undamaged. Even the white flour-like substance that coated the aspens' bark showed no sign of any disturbance. "I was at a loss what to think of it, its stroke gave sound, and therefore must have substance. These two Meteors were, perhaps, compressed bodies of phosphoric air, but without the least heat, for had there been any, the second Meteor passed so near to me I must have felt it."

David Thompson grew up in London with his Welsh mother, who probably introduced him to that culture's traditional folktales about "fairy fire," also known as will-o'-the-wisps or swamp gas. In many such stories, mischievous figures use the eerie lights to lure travelers into danger around spooky marshlands. At some point, the flames are extinguished, and the victims are left to sink into the fens.

Thompson's description of the mysterious lights he saw over Lake Susquagemow evoke will-o'-the-wisp tales from around the world. Many accounts describe their appearance as "orbs" of some form, and most modern scientists explain them as a chemical phenomenon. The notion of flammable chemicals trapped within the marshes of northern Manitoba connects logically with the natural gas now being extracted from that region. Although Thompson did not record any particular color during either of his two sightings, eyewitnesses often describe the faint blue-green and yellow-orange hues familiar from laboratory Bunsen burners. Swamp-gas accounts rarely mention noise, so it is Thompson's inclusion of those *fwaps* of jellified protoplasm against ice and aspen trees that makes his story truly memorable.

The fur agent, who grew into a solid geographer and cartographer during his long career, also gained a reputation as a master storyteller. Even though he didn't write about his experiences on Lake Susquagemow until he was approaching eighty years old, when he was plagued by failing vision and economic hardship, the details of his bizarre encounter with the diving "meteors" remained vivid. Both of the darting globes stand out in the mind of anyone reading Thompson's memoirs, as do his experiences with the much more familiar phenomenon of northern lights, or aurora borealis.

Drawing on decades of personal observations spaced across the northern tier of the continent, Thompson commented on the aurora's relative weakness along the shores of Hudson Bay and west of the Rocky Mountains compared to its astonishing brightness around another fur post where he wintered on Reindeer Lake, a huge body of water that straddles today's boundary between Saskatchewan and Manitoba at around latitude fifty-seven degrees north. There, Thompson asserted, especially in the months of February and March, the entire sky regularly bathed in a bright glow.

> We seemed to be in the centre of its action, from the horizon in every direction from north to south, from east to west, the Aurora was equally bright. Sometimes, indeed often, a tremulous motion in immense sheets, slightly tinged with the colors of the Rainbow, would roll from horizon to horizon. Sometimes there would be a stillness of two minutes; the camp dogs howled with fear.

On one nighttime hunting expedition at Reindeer Lake, the brightness of the aurora allowed Thompson to shoot an owl at a range of twenty yards. But it was the warping of human senses that most interested him. "In the rapid motions of the Aurora," he wrote, "we were all persuaded that we heard them. Reason told me that I did not, but it was cool reason against sense."

His crew was so enraptured by these displays of sonorous light that Thompson could not persuade them it was an illusion caused by "the eye deceiving the ear." To prove the point, "I had my men blindfolded by turns, and then enquired of them, if they heard the rapid motions of the Aurora. They soon became sensible they did not." Such logic could only override their senses momentarily, however, and as soon as Thompson removed the blindfolds, "so powerful was the illusion of the eye on the ear, that they still believed they heard the Aurora."

Many of the men and families who worked with Thompson had roots in the Cree culture, and he recorded their interpretation of the aurora. "The Cree Indians of North America call them the 'Dead' by the name of *Jee pe ak*, (the souls of the dead), and when the Aurora is bright in vivid graceful motion, they exclaim, See how happy our fathers are tonight, they are dancing to the enlivening songs of the other world."

Thompson, who might have preferred a more scientific explanation of the dancing lights, occasionally applied the word "meteor" to an aurora event, at least on some level comparing Reindeer Lake's wavering curtains with Lake Susquagemow's phosphoric globes of swamp gas. "This [auroral] Meteor seems to affect the great bodies of fresh water, over which they are seen more or less splendid every winter and during the summer seasons every clear night they are visible in the north eastern part of the sky." He did not, however, raise the possibility that the jellified sounds he heard as he watched the orbs over Lake Susquagemow slap into ice or trees might have been caused by the same sort of sensory distortion that he tried to explain to his men. Instead, he put forth a series of questions about the aurora at Reindeer Lake that atmospheric scientists have spent much of the last two centuries trying to work out.

What is the cause that this place seems to be
in the centre of the most vivid brightness and
extension of the Aurora?
From whence this immense extent of electric
fluid?
How is it formed?
Whither does it go?

Above the Earth

It's been several years now since I received my first personal
message from outer space. It took the form of an e-mail with
the suffix of nasa.gov and included an attached photograph that
took forever to open. When the image finally unfurled, I saw a
pleasant-looking gent in a dark polo shirt, holding up a copy of
a book I had written about David Thompson. Behind his shoulder, a porthole framed a view of cirrus clouds spread across a
patch of blue Earth that looked very far away. "I'm writing to let
you know," the message began, "that your book has been doing
some traveling." The message was signed "John Phillips, NASA
Astronaut aboard the International Space Station," an address
that transported me back to the pulp science-fiction stories and
B space movies of my youth.

But John Phillips was real. Over the next few months, he
corresponded with me while he circled our planet over and over
again, occasionally wiring me photographs of landmark lakes
along David Thompson's fur trade routes west of the Rocky
Mountains—the same area where I lived and worked. When
Phillips returned to Earth, his travels brought him to the Inland
Northwest, and we continued our conversation in person.

Phillips grew up in New York State and the Southwest. His
dad was a flying buff who spent many hours touring his kids

through local airports to marvel at the bodies and engines of different aircraft. After graduating from the Naval Academy with degrees in math and Russian, Phillips became a Navy pilot in 1974, but even as he flew jets from bases on land and sea, he always kept one eye lifted toward space. When NASA turned down his first application to be an astronaut, he tried again. And again. He realized that he needed a broader skill set if he was going to get into orbit, and left the Navy to pursue an advanced degree in space plasma physics at UCLA. From there he went on to work at New Mexico's Los Alamos National Laboratory for nine years until NASA accepted him into the space program.

When I showed David Thompson's writings about the two "meteors" at Lake Susquagemow to Phillips, he shrugged them off as swamp gas or good old will-o'-the-wisp—a purely chemical effect. He found Thompson's aurora experiences around Reindeer Lake much more alluring, however, because during his graduate studies, Phillips had focused on the sun and space environment. There he came to understand the aurora as a plasma phenomenon in which energized electrons collide with gas particles to produce light effects. He traced the discipline's growing awareness of a correlation between periods of increased sunspot activity, aurora sightings, and changes in magnetic compass readings on Earth. He described the current understanding of the global aurora as two dynamic, undulating ovals of light centered over Earth's magnetic poles.

Phillips recalled that one evening during his tenure at Los Alamos, a massive solar disturbance pushed a lobe of the northern hemisphere's auroral oval deep into the Southwest. He mistook the resulting angry red glow on the horizon for a grass fire until he realized that he was experiencing a diffuse red aurora produced by a large geomagnetic storm, rather than the curtains of green that are most often seen.

Even though Phillips usually displays a scientist's analytical mind, he can appreciate the poetry of a moment—this is a man who carried Walt Whitman's *Leaves of Grass* into space. "The first time I saw the passage you sent me about Thompson blindfolding his men to test the true effects of the aurora, it immediately reminded me of Odysseus," Phillips said. "The way he stuffed wax in the ears of his crewmen, then ordered them to tie him up tight to the forward mast of his ship so that when they sailed past the rocks where the Sirens sang, he could writhe in the total experience." It's the Greeks' own story about watching their ancestors dance, and of singing the body electric; it's the irresistible lure that connects curious spirits over time.

Phillips's natural curiosity helped him to thrive on the rigors of NASA's training regime. One exercise devoted to severe weather skills took place in the dead of winter in northern Alberta, and it involved living in an old-fashioned canvas wall tent while wearing all-wool gear. It was at this camp that Phillips first saw the vivid, graceful action of the aurora at its most sublime.

Around 2002, Phillips hit the north country again when he was assigned to prepare for a future mission of the International Space Station. He and cosmonaut Sergei Krikalev participated in an odyssey of training sessions at various Russian facilities, one of them located deep in a larch forest west of Moscow, at the same high latitude as Reindeer Lake. Three years later, a well-prepared Commander Krikalev and Flight Engineer Phillips formed the crew of the ISS's Expedition 11.

In total, the pair orbited Earth over twenty-five hundred times between April and September of 2005. The station's pathway sliced across the planet at a continuous angle, like a spiral peel off an apple, topping out at latitude fifty-one and a half degrees in both the Northern and Southern Hemispheres. The craft attained a maximum speed of more than seventeen thousand miles per hour, and its altitude varied from about two hundred and fifty to three hundred and fifty nautical miles above Earth—not nearly high enough, Phillips pointed out, to see the entire planet isolated in space. Instead, he and Krikalev observed ever-changing vistas, often recognizing familiar details, of their shared home.

All told, their journey covered over seventy million miles. During the course of the trip, John Phillips became one of the most senior American space travelers, with a total of almost two hundred days aloft. Since his mission flew through summer in the Northern Hemisphere, Phillips did not have much chance of observing a strong aurora borealis. Instead, he was able to study the aurora australis of the Southern Hemisphere winter. Orbiting the earth every ninety minutes, he often saw some trace of the aurora. "If I could get to the viewing port right as the ISS cut over Tasmania or New Zealand, and looked beyond them into the Southern Ocean, the effects were there," Phillips said. "Usually we had to glance at a downward angle to see the aurora, but occasionally we would pass directly through it."

Experience had taught him that the auroral oval is brightest just inside its perimeter. If you are standing on Earth near Reindeer Lake, and there happens to be an intense episode of geomagnetic storms, you are likely to witness bright-green sheets "dancing" just as the Cree described. Sometimes the intensity of the light can overload the sensory receptors of your brain, where neurons built for sight and hearing lie very close together. As the visual input from the aurora spills across both types of neurons, you believe that you are hearing as well as seeing the northern lights. That is the same kind of synesthesia that Thompson and his fur trade crew experienced, and may account for the "tossed jelly" sounds that he described at Lake Susquagemow.

If, on the other hand, you are on a spacecraft orbiting Earth, you have a very wide field of view that extends for many hundreds of miles. That slows the cycle way down. When the craft passes through an aurora or straight over it, observers on board usually detect only a diffuse green color, as if they were inside a pale cloud. On the ISS, Phillips found that he had to look askance, toward Earth's horizon, to see the bright coherent sheets. Even then, because of the great distance, they appeared to vibrate on a very slow period of activity. The color patterns would remain static for fifteen seconds or more before reconstituting themselves into some new form, then hold still for several more beats. "After a while, it wasn't that big of a deal," Phillips said. "With the aurora, it all depends on where you are."

On the Ground

Whenever the northern limits of the space station's orbit were above western Canada during daylight hours, John Phillips found himself in a perfect position to observe the geography of David Thompson's western journeys among the tributaries of the upper Columbia River. These conditions occurred about every forty-eight hours. The astronaut began to time breaks in his required duties so that he could return to the single viewing port that looked directly down on the planet. From that vantage, just as the ISS was approaching its maximum northern latitude for a particular swing, Phillips soon located several of

Thompson's touchstone waterways—lured to them, really, by their luminous reflections.

As the ISS passed over southeastern British Columbia, Phillips spotted the two source lakes of the West's great river, partially obscured by scudding clouds. Two days later, there he was again, leaning against his porthole, willing to coast through many more orbits in order to see the scene clearly. When his camera finally captured those twin lakes to his satisfaction, Phillips forwarded the image to me through the electric fluid of space.

Two centuries earlier, following the advice of Kootenai tribal elders, David Thompson built his first trade house west of the Rockies at the north end of those source lakes. In an attempt to absorb that landscape, I had walked myself foot-sore retracing his meanders along ancient Kootenai trails. But John Phillips's photograph instantly provided me with a much deeper sense of context. Time and space seemed to move within it, providing a taste of the slow collision of one tectonic plate against another during the Late Cretaceous period, around seventy million years ago. I could suddenly see how the uplift of the Rocky Mountains related to the long narrow trench where the Columbia flowed north along the range's western flank.

The photograph also captured the scars of more recent geologic events, after the great ice sheet of the Pleistocene epoch bulldozed along that trench from the north. As the ice retreated, it left behind a moraine of gravel that bulged just enough to nestle two puddles within the ditch, then pulled the water that leaked out of them north, in the direction of the receding glacier.

When I placed one of David Thompson's maps next to Phillips's image, all the same elements marched across the page, from the mountain ridges on each side of the nascent

Columbia's valley to the low divide that allowed the Kootenay River to rush south while its mother river began a much longer journey in the opposite direction. Thompson, with only tribal information and his own survey data, had created a bird's-eye view that jibed remarkably well with the camera's stark image.

John Phillips followed that first photo with several more, working his way south and west from the Columbia's source lakes to track the course of David Thompson's trade routes. What the astronaut saw from the space station was a landscape just below the southern edge of the great ice sheet—a terrain that at the end of the last glacial period was created and re-created by cycles of advancing ice thousands of feet thick. As those cycles waxed, ice-penned drainages backed up into huge lakes; as they waned, a succession of catastrophic meltdowns unleashed sudden torrential floods to rush across the Columbia Basin to the Pacific Ocean.

Such events seem to bend the elemental rules of physics in some of the same ways that David Thompson wrestled with during his winters in the north country. The air around us may light up with a glowing electrical charge. Fire can burble out of nowhere in the form of luminescent globes. The rocks of this Earth travel of their own accord, then explode or fly away. Ice sculpts solid ground, only to be followed by a rolling tsunami that transforms an entire landscape. The best any observer can hope for is to try to take it all in. There will be time later to figure out what was left behind and what has changed forever.

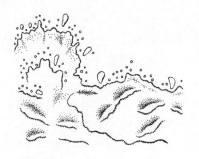

II
MELTDOWN

Keeping Fish Cool

Just north of downtown Spokane, Washington, a rough basalt mesa floats above the grid of city streets like an aerial island. Its heights provide stunning views of the Spokane and Little Spokane Rivers as they circle toward their confluence downstream. Farmed fields spot its interior, and tribal history tells of epic horse races across its flat top.

It was a searing summer day when I visited the base of the mesa with a group of Spokane tribal friends, descendants of the original residents of this area. On the edge of a quiet neighborhood, we parked near a stand of cattails that marked a small spring. A couple of younger members hopped out and dashed through a tangle of Douglas-firs, stumbling over rocks as they disappeared into the greenery. Before long, we could hear their voices oohing and aahing.

"What are we waiting for?" one of the elders asked, beckoning for me to help her out of the van.

Four of the ladies were over eighty, but they all negotiated a branchy trail that led to the base of an overgrown talus slope. We soon came in sight of an erect bus-sized boulder of pillow basalt poised higher on the hillside. "Like a finger," I heard one of them say from behind me. "Pointing the way."

Below the trail, in a hollow that had obviously been excavated and reworked by humans over the years, we found the youngsters holding out their palms in front of a crack in a craggy basalt face. The vent was only a couple of feet tall and half as wide, but even from a distance of several yards we could feel cool air wafting from its blackness. Nearby, a recent windstorm had partially toppled a gnarled, rockbound fir tree. From around its exposed roots, the same refreshing breeze poured out, continuous and strong. On such an uncomfortably hot day, it felt as though we had been carried to an entirely different place.

A search around the hollow revealed another crack that also breathed cool air. Noticeably caved in around the edges, this fissure looked as if it once might have been large enough for a person to walk inside. Craning forward, one of the ladies remarked that the subterranean air felt more than refreshing: it felt cold. A closer look revealed that ice rimed a few of the stones deeper inside.

The women, none of whom had ever been to this place, muttered with excitement. This must be one of the ice caves that they had been hearing about all their lives, but had never seen. Their Spokane ancestors, like many Plateau people, had stored fish and roots in caverns like these.

Newly arrived homesteaders trying to scratch out a living here in the early twentieth century used these cavities in exactly the same way. During the dog days of July 1929, a local newspaper ran a story headlined:

SPOKANE NATURAL WONDER
GIVES FREE ICE ON HOTTEST DAYS
OUTSIDE OF CAVES BAKES WHILE INSIDE IS ICEBOX

I had brought along a photocopy of the article for reference, and we studied the two grainy pictures that accompanied it. In the first, Mr. and Mrs. Edward Peterson posed in front of a narrow cave entrance, the opening of which looked like a tidier version of the vent beside which we were standing. The couple gazed at a thermometer that registered forty-five degrees, even as the rest of Spokane reported ninety-seven. Mrs. Peterson was quoted as saying that the cave extended about six feet into the hillside, and that she kept fruit inside it year-round.

By this time, the young explorers in the group had begun to work their way uphill along a pathway between the moss-covered talus slope and a windrow of loose basalt. The rest of us followed to an open area, where we gathered around a circular depression that was stuffed full with rotting lumber and rounds of old firewood. More cold air drifted from its depths.

This rubble-filled pit must be the old well described in the 1929 newspaper article, we decided. We compared the setting to the second photo, in which Edward Peterson squatted beside a rectangular cellar entrance. We soon spotted a handrail post and part of a step from Peterson's neatly framed stairway among the debris. In the photo, Peterson had just ascended from the depths of the pit, where he had plucked a piece of ice from the rock floor to share with Patsy, his German shepherd. There were always several hundred pounds of ice on the bottom of the eight-foot well, Peterson explained. Ever since his parents homesteaded the place in 1899, the family had stored meat down there.

The newspaper reporter expressed bafflement at the source of the Petersons' ice before wrapping up his article with the revelation that "Tule mats, well preserved, have been taken from this well." That fact did not surprise the Spokane women, whose elders had told them how they would line their storage pits with tule mats, then arrange twined bags filled with salmon or roots between layers of sage leaves to discourage probing animals. In multifamily caches, distinct designs woven into each bag made for easy identification. Leaning over the edge of the pit, the women wondered whether any more of their ancestors' tule mats or storage bags might still be down there, hidden in the darkness among the rocks—still perfectly flexible in the moist air, still carrying an odor of dried fish that no passage of time could extinguish.

At some point in the 1950s, residents in the neighborhood grew concerned about children playing among the dangerous rocks. They collapsed the cave openings and filled Peterson's well with waste wood, but judging from the air that was caressing our faces, its bottom must still be covered with ice.

As we enjoyed our respite, one of the ladies recalled a cave that her uncle had told her about, somewhere near Kettle Falls. When he was about five years old, he had gone with his parents to the great salmon fishery there, a few years before the construction of Grand Coulee Dam. While everyone else was busy with the fish, he wandered off, tracing the edge of a stony outcrop. After a while he felt a breath of cool breeze seeping from a crack. Squeezing between two rocks, he found himself inside a cave. There he saw big icicles hanging down. He recalled touching the cold daggers and feeling the magic that made them grow. He broke one off and licked it: the first Popsicle he ever had.

"Just like here," his niece said, leaning her head into the cool flow of air. "If we could crawl down into this hole, there would be Popsicles waiting for us."

Many early newspapers and oral traditions throughout the Northwest contained reports about "ice caves," "ice wells," "ice tunnels," "old ice," and "blue ice" that mirrored the conditions of the odd vents in Spokane. In the days before electricity, such features were commonly used for refrigeration. In the town of Thompson Falls, Montana, on the Clark Fork River, early white settlers discovered that their basements often tapped into "cold air wells" that were perfect for preserving meat and produce. When a 1950s-era dam across Cabinet Gorge raised the water table upstream, it changed the dynamics of those drafty basements, and many old-timers were forced to purchase their first refrigerators. As recently as the 1980s, a road crew widening the state highway in the vicinity uncovered chunks of "ground ice" while removing rock from the base of surrounding outcrops. At the time, some reporters of the discovery wondered if the frozen blocks might be ancient ice left behind in the wake of the last glaciers.

Wondering whether all these accounts might be related, I contacted Idaho geologist Roy Breckinridge, who has spent much of his career thinking about ice. We visited the vents and well at the foot of the mesa in Spokane, and stumbled across talus slopes along the Clark Fork River. I asked him if the road crew could possibly have dug into a pocket of glacial ice. "I don't think so," he replied. "I think they exposed new ice."

He then patiently explained how each ice cave, shattered out-crop, and scree slide harbors its own peculiarities, depending upon the different sizes and shapes of the rocks and their placement in relation to each other.

In situations where air has enough room to flow through the spaces between the rocks, a sub-surface area can function much like a modern heat pump. Breezes can circulate in a cooling pattern and sink into a cavity that stores them in a passive sump. As air rises back through this natural system, it can combine with humidity to manufacture ice. All these configurations, for a geologist like Breckenridge, can be linked to earth-building processes of long ago. The question becomes which combination of natural forces arranged the rocks in just such a way to create these natural iceboxes. The answers to questions like this are rarely simple.

Imagining the Deluge

Roy Breckenridge is part of a long tradition of geologists, both amateur and professional, who have attempted to explain certain anomalies in the Inland Northwest landscape. In the 1920s, some of them focused on the extent of the Cordilleran Ice Sheet during the last ice age, and how that ice related to an array of features that stretch from western Montana across the Columbia Basin and beyond.

The Pleistocene story line at that time held that one lobe of the great ice sheet had pushed south at least as far as the Spokane River. A local geologist named Thomas Largé created a map that showed its cold tongue licking against the mesa where the Petersons lived. The power of that ice would have scraped and shattered rocks all along the mesa's base; as the tongue retreated, it would have left behind erratic boulders and massive windrows of debris. Largé proposed that ripple marks and scoured volcanic flows throughout the vicinity were the result of meltwater pushed to high velocities under the weight of the retreating ice lobe. Many established geologists agreed with his ideas.

University of Chicago professor J Harlen Bretz, however, was not convinced of that theory and spent years combing the dry side of Washington State, carefully examining and reexamining the evidence. He came to believe that the ice stopped well north of Spokane, and that many of the distinctive features of the Inland Northwest were not the result of the slow advance and retreat of glaciers, but rather had been sculpted by a sudden massive flood. Harlen Bretz was not the first to entertain the notion of water as a major player in the drama. A century earlier, naturalist David Douglas and missionary Samuel Parker had both surmised that the Grand Coulee west of Spokane must have been carved by some dramatic flow. In 1899, geologist and forester J. B. Leiberg postulated that an ice plug had dammed the Clark Fork River near its mouth on Lake Pend Oreille. In 1910, another geologist, J. T. Pardee, reckoned that this ice dam must have attained a thickness of several thousand feet. He visualized how it would have impounded tributaries all the way upstream to Flathead Lake and the Bitterroot Valley, creating a vast body of water that he called Glacial Lake Missoula.

Pardee's work helped Harlen Bretz to envision a credible mechanism for a flood of biblical scale, and in 1923, Bretz published the first of more than a dozen technical papers detailing his ideas. He theorized that as the climate warmed at the end of the Pleistocene, the ice dam had come apart. Its sudden failure allowed the totality of the lake's water to flush the ice from Lake Pend Oreille's basin, then fan out with devastating speed, crashing through the Spokane countryside and across the Columbia Basin.

The deluge backed up behind the constriction of Wallula Gap before tearing through the Columbia River Gorge with renewed force. This single jet of floodwater split again at the Willamette Valley, forking to find separate ways to the sea.

Few of Harlen Bretz's fellow geologists bought into the notion of the cataclysmic event that he called the Spokane or Lake Missoula Flood, and decades passed before the theory gained wide acceptance. But by the early twenty-first century, the saga of the Ice Age floods stood as a defining chapter in the region's history. To gain any sense of the Inland Northwest landscape, you have to comprehend these immense forces at work. You must try and picture how the dam failed within a matter of hours, and how the whole event played out over the course of a few days. You have to realize that, after the first apocalyptic deluge, global weather cycled back toward the cold. Within a few decades, a lobe of the continental glacier again crept south to form another thick dam across the Clark Fork delta and Lake Pend Oreille. A new Glacial Lake Missoula filled, lapping at levels clearly visible today on bare hillsides. Another warming trend and catastrophic ice failure followed, releasing another torrent to pound its way to the sea. You have to imagine this happening dozens of times as the climate wobbled toward the warmth of the Holocene epoch. Today we have accepted the spectacle of these floods washing over our earth as common knowledge, and we marvel that it took geologists so long to figure it out.

Inside the Icebox

Even though the basics of this story have been available for almost a century, the devil, as Roy Breckenridge continually points out, is in the details. He and his colleagues study the events that took place around Lake Pend Oreille and the lower Clark Fork River at the end of the Pleistocene, trying to figure out how the Cordilleran Ice Sheet formed a wall that was tall enough and strong enough to back up an enormous Glacial Lake Missoula. They want to know how such a massive dam could have failed so catastrophically, and exactly what happened when three thousand square miles of deep water roared away. They are curious as to how the ice then re-formed to replay the same scene, with subtle variations, many times over.

Sometimes scaling down to the finer points of the story, all the way to refrigerated basements and cold air wells, can provide insight. And sometimes you have to consider the much grander progression of deep time.

As dinosaurs roamed the earth during the Cretaceous epoch, around a hundred million years ago, a massive island terrane docked against the western edge of North America and then slowly pulled away, creating a long valley that emerges from British Columbia's Kootenay Lake, follows a brief run of river across the border into Idaho, then crosses a gentle divide into the Clark Fork–Pend Oreille drainage. This valley is known to geologists as the Purcell Trench. During the Miocene epoch, more than twenty million years ago, a river flowed through the trench, cutting a meandering course through less resistant rock exposures and fault zones.

Much more recently, at the end of the Pleistocene, the Purcell Lobe of the Cordilleran Ice Sheet moved down the pathway of the Purcell Trench, filling the ancestral valley occupied today by Lake Pend Oreille. When this frozen river pushed through the basin, it collided with Green Monarch Ridge on the eastern rim. Forged from some of the oldest rocks on the continent—the ancient Belt bedrock of the Mesoproterozoic era—Green Monarch provided a solid terminal buttress for the ice. As the glacier continued to advance, more and more ice piled up behind the ridge, gradually thickening into the dam that created the first of a series of Glacial Lake Missoulas. Geologists who have studied the dams that developed at this site maintain that whenever the depth of Lake Missoula approached 2,000 feet, the water's sheer weight began to compromise the ice cleaving to the base of Green Monarch Ridge. Small cracks began to appear, and streams of water flowed into the cracks, boring tunnels beneath the ice plug. The combined forces from the weight of the dam and the volume of Lake Missoula pressurized the water flowing into these tunnels so that the pathways enlarged very quickly. Jets of water churning along Green Monarch's solid wall undermined the dam and caused its sudden failure. (YouTube videos monitoring the removal of modern concrete dams attest to the power of this process.)

After the last glacier retreated, Lake Pend Oreille remained. Today it is recognized as the largest and deepest body of water in the Idaho Panhandle. Its natural surface level lies about 2,050 feet above sea level; the ice-carved mountains that surround it reach to 6,000 feet and more. Its waters plunge as much as 1,150 feet deep along its southern reach. During his investigations around the lake, one question that intrigued Roy Breckinridge was whether such great depth was the result of the grinding ice sheet or the repeated slashing floods. Although the carving power of glaciers is well documented, some geologists contended that the pressurized water shooting from the ice dams would have eaten away enough bedrock to significantly deepen Lake Pend Oreille.

Breckinridge believed that the answer might lie on the bottom of the lake. He knew that the most dynamic part of a glacier is its forward toe, which makes both first and last contact with raw ground. That is where the ice's bulldozing power performs its most drastic razing of the landscape. Since the ice lobe that filled the Pend Oreille basin would have repeatedly gouged its southern edge, and since the main discharges of Glacial Lake Missoula would have been ripped through that same area, Breckenridge and his team were drawn to the lake's southern arm. The sediments there, they reasoned, might well show the difference between what had been sculpted by ice and what had been eroded by floods.

By chance, during World War II the US Navy had established a training base along the southwestern edge of the lake, exactly where the floodwaters had once poured out. Although this station was decommissioned in 1946, the Navy understood the advantages of retaining a secluded site with quiet deep water and, over the years, it developed a research unit there that regularly performs acoustic experiments with small ships and submarines.

Breckenridge learned that naval technicians had constructed a sonic profile of the lake bathymetry by towing acoustic sources through the water, broadcast at different levels and captured by hydrophone receivers. Although the military project focused on the lake bottom's shallowest sediments, Breckenridge guessed that their comprehensive data might also have something to say about the bedrock below them.

The Navy's seismic data for the lake's southern arm showed gradual slopes dropping off the east and west shores, but the east side alone was marked by a stark subsurface bench running directly down the lake from Green Monarch Ridge. This underwater bench, as well as a similar one still visible above lake level today, can be interpreted as the result of the tunneling jets of water that disintegrated the ice dam.

The naval data also revealed distinct stratigraphic units of debris on the lake bottom. Breckenridge believes that the deepest and thickest of these layers correspond to sediments left behind after the most recent ice-dam failure. Beneath that debris, the sonar outlined a classic U-shaped bedrock basin with a nearly flat center—the shape that defines glacier-carved valleys all over the world. Furthermore, the actual bottom of the lake was much deeper than he had anticipated. Along its south arm, the lake level of 2,050 feet, combined with a water depth of 1,150 feet, means that the top sediment layer lies 900 feet above sea level. Naval bathymetry showed that the depth of the bedrock basin approaches an astonishing 700 feet *below* sea level. This means that 1,600 feet of sediments rest below the water. In other words, the sediments themselves are much deeper than the deepest water in the lake.

While the hydrologic forces of high-pressure tunneling beneath an ice mass can reach impressive speeds, no model or study has shown that they can generate enough power to carve bedrock to any great extent below sea level. Breckenridge determined that the bottom of Lake Pend Oreille is actually an overdeepened glaciated basin that has been refilled with the debris of numerous Ice Age floods. It was created in much the same way as well-studied elongate lake valleys in British Columbia, glacier-carved valleys in the Alps, and coastal fjords in Norway. "So," concluded Breckinridge, "those ice caves, which Largé thought were created by the glaciers, were in fact formed by the big floods. And the bottom of Lake Pend Oreille, which many geologists believed must have been dredged by the floods, was actually carved by ice."

Flowing through the Country

After the last of the Lake Missoula floods passed down the Columbia to the sea, vegetation sprouted on the massive gravel dumps and sand bars left in its wake. Mammoths and camels returned to browse their former haunts, and anadromous fish swam back upstream to spawn. People were there with them, spreading back across the landscape as conditions allowed.

The first written descriptions and accurate maps of this reclaimed world were forged by fur agent David Thompson. When Thompson surveyed his way from the Rockies to the Pacific between 1807 and 1812, he carefully plotted each new drainage that he entered, taking countless sextant shots and compass bearings. One of his maps depicts the interlaced rivulets formed by the Clark Fork River's delta at the northeast corner of Lake Pend Oreille—the site of the ice dam that impounded Glacial Lake Missoula. Mountain ridges crawl across the landscape, marking the drainage divides for all the surrounding rivers and outlining the limits of Lake Missoula's expanse upstream along the Clark Fork to Missoula and south through the Bitterroot Valley, as well as east and north up the Flathead River through the Mission Valley to Flathead Lake.

Thompson often traveled with tribal guides, who showed him the most efficient way to get from one place to the next. As he trekked across the region multiple times, he observed how local people circled through their known world to gather essential resources. Because of Thompson's close attention, it is possible to trace the ways in which the Plateau peoples of the early nineteenth century fit into the landscape shaped by the Ice Age floods.

When paddling on Lake Pend Oreille near modern Sandpoint, Idaho, Thompson set his course—undoubtedly with the help of his Kalispel guide—by a distinctive rock that marks the narrowing of the river as it leaves the lake. This knoll, now known as Tank Hill, was stripped bare by the Ice Age floods, creating a landmark that served as a beacon for travelers on the lake and on land. The roiling waters dropped a pendant bar of gravel on Tank Hill's downstream side; this lode of handy aggregate has served as a commercial pit for many years, providing the road gravel that transformed many of the tribal trails that Thompson traveled into modern highways.

When the fur agent journeyed southwest from the Pend Oreille to the Spokane drainage, his guides directed him to a trail that followed the path of the deluge as it burst from Lake Pend Oreille's southern basin and overran a low divide, where it dropped sediments on a plain known today as Rathdrum Prairie. Bars of flood gravel there created several small lakes that appear on Thompson's maps. He recorded how water flowing from one of these pocket lakes, instead of following the expected stream course to the Spokane River, "disappears" into hundreds of feet of porous flood deposits.

In the spring of 1812, Thompson led a horse brigade along the north bank of the Spokane River. Where the river bent south to crash through a series of formidable falls that today mark the city's center, he and his voyageurs followed a tribal trail west across grasslands spotted with well-spaced ponderosa pines. The brigade was heading for an ancient fishing village nine miles downstream from the falls, where a handful of Thompson's men had built the Spokane House fur trading post two seasons before. In a typically terse daybook entry along the way, he marked his course by "a range of Knowls to our Right."

A knoll to Thompson meant a distinct feature, often rocky, and the one he sighted as he cruised through what is now north Spokane was a distinct circular mesa, fairly flat on top, that had been carved and recarved by successive Ice Age floods. Thompson took advantage of the open parkland around the southern edge of the knoll to trot his horses straight through to Spokane House. From that outpost, more dotted lines on his large map trace tribal trails through flood coulees of the Cheney-Palouse scablands all the way south to the Snake River.

The coarse gravels that form the beds of the Spokane and Little Spokane Rivers, dropped there by subtle flow changes in the last of the Lake Missoula floods, cover a range of sizes. For untold generations, several species of trout, as well as steelhead and salmon, thrashed their tails in these gravels to form redds for laying eggs. The fish nourished local people and visitors from far away—including David Thompson, who upon arriving at Spokane House in spring 1812 found "all well, they have these 2 days caught many Trout."

For the past thirteen thousand years, features carved by the Ice Age floods have shaped the way people live in and move across a large swath of the Inland Northwest landscape. The deluge may read like a signature origin myth to someone from the outside, but for anyone who travels along the many paths gouged by ice or swept clear by rushing water, each detail of the story points to a practical reality: from Mesoproterozoic time to the Pleistocene, from the sweep of open landscape to the range of a single plant species, from the frenzy of spawning fish to the continuous trickle of new people who have filtered into the region since the floods receded, from the breadth of Grand Coulee to a cool cavern just wide enough to slide into, and just right for storing food.

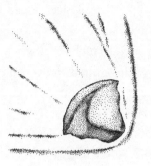

III
The Longest Journey

An Intelligent Farmer

This is a story about a rock that flew. One thread of the tale begins in Oregon with a pioneer farmer named Ellis Hughes, who worked a small parcel of pleasantly rolling land southeast of Portland between the hamlets of West Linn and Willamette, near the border of present-day Clackamas County. On a November day in 1902, Hughes was walking home from cutting firewood for the Willamette grade school when he spotted part of a rusty crosscut saw blade about fifty feet off his path. No one wasted valuable steel in those days, so he ventured into the woods for a closer look. There he found the saw piece resting against a large "metallic-looking rock protruding above the ground." Nestled within a grove of recently cut stumps, the greater portion of the mass was buried in the earth. A thicket of hazel bushes helped to mask its presence from the trail.

Something about this boulder piqued Hughes's curiosity, and the next day he brought his neighbor Bill Dale to the spot. "I sat down on the rock," Hughes recounted. "It was about one and a half feet above the ground and very flat." Bill Dale quickly realized this was no ordinary stone. "Hughes," said Dale, "have you seen this rock before?"

"Yes," Hughes answered. "I saw it yesterday." He leaned down to pick up a handy white cobble and hammered on the outcrop. It rang like a bell.

"Hughes," Dale said, upon hearing those clear tones, "I'll bet this is a meteor."

Betting on a meteor—or meteorite, because it was definitely on Earth, not in space—was not such a long shot in that time and place. As early as 1856, a geologist exploring in Oregon's southwest corner sent samples of what he thought might be a large meteorite to a Boston chemist for analysis. Assays confirmed his guess, leading to a succession of searchers who tried unsuccessfully to relocate that find. Another southern Oregon resident caused a buzz when he fished a fifteen-pound aerolite, or stony meteorite, out of a creek in 1894. That happened to be the same year that Arctic explorer and savvy self-promoter Robert Peary made a visit to Greenland. There, Cape York Inuit guided him to their traditional source of iron for tools, which turned out to be a massive iron meteorite. For the next three years, the explorer's crew struggled to collect three rough chunks to deliver to the American Museum of Natural History in New York. The largest piece of that trio was shaped roughly like a tent and figured prominently in an important Cape York cultural story. Ignoring this age-old connection, Peary dubbed it with the nonsense name of Ahnighito. He declared it to be the largest meteorite ever mounted for exhibition, and in fact, it retains its heavyweight title of more than thirty tons to this day. The museum eventually purchased it from Peary's widow for $40,000.

Ellis Hughes and Bill Dale might well have read one of the many popular accounts describing Peary's profitable adventure, and the Oregon pair certainly held similar ambitious goals. The thirty-seven-year-old Hughes had grown up in Wales, where people seem to inherit a close knowledge of mining, and he had worked in Australian mines along the way to his West Linn farmstead. Bill Dale was a traveling prospector of the same breed, and his relationship with Ellis Hughes was close enough that some contemporary accounts described him as boarding in the Hughes household. One reporter stated that "together they roamed over the hills seeking minerals;" another identified them as "a couple of prospectors who thought at first they had uncovered a big vein of iron."

After considerable digging and some preliminary assay work, Hughes and Dale "soon learned that their rocky mass was indeed iron, but also discovered that it was an isolated block and a meteorite instead of a 'reef' upon which could be located a great mine, as they supposed at first." They also determined that the land surrounding their lodestone was owned by the Oregon Iron and Steel company.

This local company had a checkered history that stretched back to the 1860s, when investors constructed the first iron smelting furnace west of the Mississippi to process a brown hematite ore quarried at nearby Lake Oswego. To fuel its smelter, Oregon Iron and Steel had acquired timbered properties that could supply cordwood for making charcoal. Although by 1902 their furnace had lain cold for several years, Hughes and Dale had no wish to generate any excitement, and so moved cautiously. They covered the meteorite with dirt and brush, then attempted to purchase the acreage from the company as common farmland. To finance the deal, Bill Dale traveled to eastern Oregon, where he hoped to sell the rights to one of his mining claims near Baker City. Although his name appeared as the meteorite's discoverer in a few subsequent newspaper articles, he apparently never returned to Clackamas County.

Hughes remained on the farm with his family. After a few weeks, they gave up on Dale but not on the stone. "My wife had ideas," Hughes later said. "She was afraid somebody would go up and get it the next day." Although sharing the concern of his wife, Phebe, the Welshman crafted a plan that required a bit more patience, and waited for the winter rains to ease before setting his scheme into motion.

To begin, he blazed a road about eight hundred feet in the wrong direction, so that his neighbors would not catch on to his game. He then spent several months in the spring and summer of 1903 cutting a direct path between his house and the meteorite. Next, the resourceful ex-miner constructed "an ingenious car with log body-timbers and sections of tree trunks as wheels." In late summer, relying only upon Phebe, their fifteen-year-old son, and a horse for assistance, he embarked on an odyssey of practical engineering.

After clearing away his brushy camouflage from the previous fall, Hughes positioned his cart downhill, set up a series of jackscrews, and began, inch by inch, to raise the stone. As the meteorite slowly emerged from its hole, he blocked the tilted side progressively higher until it overbalanced and flopped onto his makeshift truck. "It couldn't have been done better if you'd laid it there with your own hands," he recounted years later, still savoring the moment.

Hughes and son secured their cargo to the cart, then used more chains to anchor a capstan into position about a hundred feet down their rough-hewn road. Known to local loggers as a "Spanish windlass," this contraption consisted of a stout section of log mounted upright and fixed with perpendicular spokes to turn it. According to Hughes, it was all constructed out of whatever "hash" he found lying around the house. He rigged a system of heavy ropes, pulley blocks, and a hundred feet of wire cable between cart and capstan, then encouraged his horse to plod around in circles, drawing the heavily burdened cart forward. Each length of the cable lurched around the capstan inch by torturous inch, and many hours were spent locked motionless behind the myriad stumps of the smelter company's woodlot. With more than half a mile of open ground between their starting point and the safety of home, Hughes estimated that the greatest distance gained in any one day never exceeded seventy-five feet. When autumn rains turned the rough path into mud, the team laid down a track of sawn planks and carried on. It was mid-October before they had the finish line in sight.

By that time, word had leaked out that the Hughes family had found a meteorite. A newspaperman came nosing around the planked section of the road, but Hughes covered his cart with gunnysacks and kept his mouth shut. When the reporter asked Hughes point-blank to uncover the prize, he flatly refused. "I told him the sun might warp it," he recalled with a twinkle in his eye.

Portland resident A. W. Miller—"a student of geology, mineralogy, meteorology, and other ologies"—was initially dubious upon hearing rumors of the discovery, telling one journalist that in spite of overblown stories, no verified meteorite had ever been found in the Pacific Northwest. He cited a recent incident that began with a blaze of light across the night sky, then people near Lake Oswego claiming to have found pieces of an exploded meteorite. Called upon to assess one of the fragments, Miller found that it "proved to be only a bit of slag from the iron works there."

Despite his skepticism, Miller relayed the news from Willamette to his contacts at the Smithsonian Institution, and a staff geologist there wrote back, encouraging him to visit the site. When Miller reached the Hughes place, he "was not able to secure much information of value," according to an interview in the Portland *Morning Oregonian*. "The 'meteor' was covered in sacks and wraps and he did not feel at liberty to disturb it much."

But no number of gunnysacks could hide the fact that there was more to the story. "There is some dispute as to the proprietorship of the mass," continued the article. "The land on which it was found by Mr. Hughes is claimed by another and an effort is being made to move it onto the ground of Mr. Hughes. It may be imagined that the situation is strained."

Neither the strained situation nor the rude sack camouflage kept Miller from ruminating about the stone's net worth. "Iron is worth about 1 cent a pound and nickel about 3 cents," he told the newspaper reporter, "but as a meteor its value depends upon who wants it and how badly it is wanted."

The Smithsonian Institution wanted the stone badly enough to reroute its specimen collector F. W. Crosby from fieldwork in California. Upon his arrival in Willamette, Crosby was able to convince Hughes to allow a quick examination of the object in question. After some preliminary pounding with his rock hammer, the collector commented on the meteorite's iron content, some distinct pits caused by heat as it passed through the atmosphere, and a rusted surface that indicated "the monster may have been buried in the hillside for many centuries."

Crosby estimated that the stone would weigh between ten and twenty tons, far larger than any in the hands of the Smithsonian at that time. He then shared his opinion that "the Government alone can afford to acquire the ownership of the meteor" because of the great expense of its purchase and removal, and he conjectured that because of its enormous weight, the stone would unfortunately be of less value to its owner than if it were a quarter of its actual size.

Crosby also attracted a local shadow, in the person of Colonel L. L. Hawkins, proprietor of the free museum in Portland's city hall. Hawkins began to speculate that the meteorite would travel to the 1904 World's Fair in Saint Louis, then return to Portland for the 1905 celebration of the Lewis and Clark Centennial Exposition.

The front page of the *Morning Oregonian* of October 31 displayed a photograph of the Hughes meteorite, which looked like a magnificent breast-shaped sculpture, securely chained to its cart. HUGE METEOR FOUND NEAR OREGON CITY proclaimed the banner above the photo. LARGEST EVER FOUND IN THE UNITED STATES.

Amidst all this bustle, Ellis Hughes finally managed to winch the cumbersome cart to his property and roll the stone onto the ground. It lay on one side, with its highly eroded bottom raked up at about a forty-five-degree angle—a very good position for viewing. He erected a shed around it and attached a sign announcing a price of twenty-five cents. In those days, rail lines ran from Portland to Oregon City, and an electric streetcar extended to the settlement of Willamette. From that point, viewers had to walk the final two miles to reach the

Hughes farm, but they came in droves anyway. While gawkers had their pictures snapped in front of the papered backdrop of Hughes's shed, local pundits continued to speculate about where such a treasure might eventually land.

One report stated that Colonel Hawkins was "quite certain to secure the mass of metal for the free museum, as several directors of the Oregon Iron & Steel Company, on whose land it was found, are of the opinion that it should be placed in this museum." The foresighted Hawkins had personally visited the meteorite's original resting place on iron company land; he had also obtained a fragment of the stone, and was only waiting for expert confirmation of its authenticity before making final arrangements with company directors. "The persons who have gone to considerable labor and expense in moving the mass by means of tackles and a rude carriage on block wheels . . . have not waited to ascertain the value of it and are therefore likely to be out and injured," wrote one reporter, obviously in sympathy with Hawkins. "If the mass is simply bog iron it is of but little value. If it is a meteorite its value as a curiosity would hardly pay for transporting it any great distance." This article ended, as would many later accounts, with a twist of humor.

> The taking and carrying away of all sorts of things has become all too common in these days, but a mass of some seven tons of base metal has not been dragged half a mile before, and if the attempt to carry it away should succeed it will be necessary for anyone on whose property a meteorite shall fall in the future to see that it is not allowed to cool.

The *Oregonian* countered with a more general history of meteorite discoveries, penned by A. W. Miller. After referencing the famous Athens meteor of 476 BC and a recent schoolboy ruse involving a chunk of slag from Oregon Iron and Steel's smelting furnace, Miller expressed his belief that the size of Ellis Hughes's stone would be equal to or greater than Peary's famous Greenland find. "It is to be regretted that the monstrous mass of nickel steel near Oregon City is to become a subject for litigation and the only ones to be benefited by its discovery are likely to be the attorneys," he lamented. "Were it not for the parties who made the discovery and brought it out, it might have remained buried in its secluded spot many generations more."

Among the curious visitors who paid twenty-five cents to see the meteorite was an attorney for Oregon Iron and Steel. "He offered $50 for the whole piece, and said he wanted to show it at the Buffalo World's Fair. I wouldn't listen to him," Hughes later told an interviewer. According to one account, the lawyer backtracked along the trail that Hughes had blazed for his cart and reached the recent excavation on his employers' land. With that raw track as evidence, the company filed suit to regain possession of the meteorite. Colonel Hawkins, taking advantage of the publicity to champion his own cause, revealed that the foreman of the iron company had told him it wasn't worth hiring a crew to break up the meteorite for smelting, and that the Smithsonian had plenty of other specimens on hand. "The place where it naturally belongs is in the free museum here, and there it will doubtless be deposited."

January 1904 saw the first scientific article about the meteorite, titled "Clackamas Meteoric Iron," published in *Science*, the journal of the American Association for the Advancement of Science. Taking most of his information from A. W. Miller's report, the author speculated that the "Clackamas Iron" would rank in size with Peary's Greenland find and another famous discovery still residing in Mexico. The *Science* author had seen a photograph of the Oregon meteorite and longed to investigate its classic dome shape, elliptic base, and small pits. Obviously, much technical work remained to be done on this most promising specimen.

A Scientific Vendor

In February 1904, Professor Henry A. Ward arrived in Portland after a cross-country train trip. Seventy years old that year, Ward had been hunting geologic curiosities most of his life, supporting himself as a natural history professor, a gold miner, a dealer of curiosities, a friend of Wild Bill Cody, and an early instigator of Buffalo Bill's *Wild West Show*. Ward did possess undeniable skills: the director of the Smithsonian once introduced him as "the Napoleon of young American zoologists," and it was Ward's laboratory that stuffed and mounted P. T. Barnum's elephant, Jumbo, after the famous pachyderm was struck by a train. Now in the latter years of his career, Ward spent much of his time careening around the globe. A brief notice that appeared in a Portland paper on February 13 identified him as an "enthusiastic student collector and dealer in meteors, who is constantly on a route about as erratic as that of a meteor."

From Portland, Ward made the rail, streetcar, and pedestrian journey to view the Clackamas Iron. "Professor Ward stated that while here he had no intention of trying to secure the meteor for commercial purposes," a reporter wrote, "but as he is a buyer and seller of meteors some were afraid he might endeavor to gain possession of it to take it out of the state to sell." When questioned more pointedly, Ward denied the charge, but the journalist was far from convinced.

> [Ward] is an enthusiast on the subject of meteors, always willing to part with any he may acquire for a reasonable consideration, and some imagine that he would pluck the planets from their orbits, the stars from their sphere, tear the constellations from the skies, knock a hole in the bottom of the great dipper, sunder Gemini, hound Ursa Major from the firmament, shear Aries, put a ring in the nose of Taurus, halter Pegasus, put on exhibition the modest, retiring seventh sister of the Pleiades, yea, even change the position of the pole star if he could by so doing secure control of any of these heavenly bodies or constellations for commercial purposes. It is not likely, however, that he will obtain possession of the Oregon meteor, for the real owners of it are not liable to allow it to be taken from the state and lost to the City Museum for any sum he is likely to offer for it. They are too patriotic for that.

The ruthless enthusiast in question was at that same moment composing a detailed description of the Oregon meteorite, which he read before the Rochester Academy of Science in upstate New York on March 14, 1905. His paper, which ran to almost five thousand words and included stunning photographs, was reprinted in the July 9 edition of the *Scientific American Supplement*, capturing the attention of enthusiasts across the continent.

Ward rechristened the Clackamas Iron with the more mellifluous name of the "Willamette Meteorite." He described the slopes above the Tualatin River, where it had been buried within "a primeval forest of pines and birch" at an elevation of 380 feet above sea level. He gave a heroic account of Hughes's journey with the stone to his family farm. "It was a herculean struggle between man and meteorite, and the man conquered," wrote Ward. "It is unpleasant to have to record what followed."

After recounting the distasteful legal arguments of possession versus ownership, Ward took the pulse of local residents. "Public opinion is divided as to the probable outcome," he reported. "But sympathy lies mainly with Hughes, the finder of the mass, and the only man recorded in common life or among scientific collectors as having run away with a 14-ton meteorite."

Ward then summarized his scientific analysis. "My first work was to take full measures," he declared. The stone turned out to be a little over ten feet in length; its breadth across the base, seven feet; the vertical height to the summit of the dome, four feet; and the total circumference of the base, twenty-five feet four inches.

The professor compared the shape of the rock to a stubby cone marked with a subtle asymmetry: while a cross section through the upper dome would describe an almost-perfect circle, a slice of the lower part would present an oval form. He used the German term *brustseite* to politely convey the rock's smooth breast shape. Assuming that the apex of the dome must have formed the leading edge of the missile as it entered the atmosphere, he imagined the relentless annealing effects of terrific heat and slow cooling as it plunged to Earth. These forces would have created its consistently rounded character, even though it showed none of the fine polish or pitting he had seen on other meteorites. He wondered if some small scabs of a faintly deeper color, sprinkled randomly across the brustseite surface might be pockets of melted minerals, but he could draw no further conclusions because of the unfavorable viewing conditions. "I may be permitted to again remind the reader," wrote the professor, "that I could study the meteorite only while kneeling in the mud, holding an umbrella over my head in a heavy fall of rain and sleet, and with a temperature too cold to comfortably hold a pencil."

Ward was especially fascinated by the stone's extremely varied surface. A border that extended entirely around the meteorite's lower half was covered with small fingerprint-shaped pittings, called "piezographs," which he had seen on other aerolites. This border also contained a series of perfectly round boreholes, one to three inches in diameter and three or four inches in depth—again, similar in appearance to other meteorites. But neither Ward nor any other geologist had ever described anything like the openings that appeared on the stone's upper face: "deep, broadly open basins and broad furrows or channels cutting down deeply into the mass." The professor again theorized that these indentations must have contained nodules of some mineral, such as troilite, that was softer than the surrounding iron, and that those nodules must have melted during entry into Earth's atmosphere. Ellis Hughes, in fact, had used one such handy opening to chain the monstrous rock to his cart.

Ward then investigated the bottom of the meteorite, which Hughes had exposed when he rolled it to the ground.

We have before us a most singular and astonishing
group of concavities and caverns . . . they cross
the mass from side to side and end to end . . .

They make a confusion of kettle-holes; of wash-bowls; of small bath-tubs!

We recognize at once that we are not treating of an ordinary meteorite phenomenon. We are observing an action or effect of decomposition, carried to its more extreme degree. We are reminded of the deeply water-worn surfaces of limestone in certain caves. Of eroded blocks of gypsum; or, most of all, of the cragged protuberances of old coral rock.

The professor believed that the cavities were the result of water erosion, not a trip through space, reasoning that centuries of accumulated vegetable debris, working in the acidic environment of a Northwest rain forest, may well have encouraged this decomposition. Many visitors to Hughes's display photographed their children curled up in the little bathtubs, or their infants nestled in suitable niches. These snapshots provided the most iconic images of the Willamette Meteorite, including a pair that appeared in Ward's *Scientific American* piece.

At the end of his paper, the professor turned his attention to the deeper mysteries of the stone. From the moment of its discovery, curious onlookers had hammered at the edges of its ragged basins, breaking off chunks to carry home. Ward had collected his own souvenirs, and the *Scientific American Supplement* included a photograph of one such relic, penetrated by one of the odd boreholes and scarred with the pittings of the stone's primordial journey. His assistant in Rochester had etched its surface with acid in order to analyze the interwoven bands of molecular structure that geologists use to catalog meteorites. Ward had also sent fragments to two laboratories for chemical analysis, confirming Portland reports that the meteorite contained more than 91 percent iron and around 8 percent nickel, but adding traces of cobalt and phosphorous to the mix. "Perhaps," mused Ward, "more about the inner structure of the iron may be developed as the mass is further sectioned."

A Considered Judgment

Meanwhile, back in Oregon, time marched toward an April court date pitting Ellis Hughes against Oregon Iron and Steel. The company's lawyers had every reason to be confident, according to a legal precedent from northern Iowa. In spring 1890, a massive fireball had streaked across the skies of Winnebago County, littering the countryside with a shower of meteorite fragments. Locals picked up several hundred pieces that ranged in weight from a few ounces to eighty-one pounds. A Minnesota geologist, hearing of the incident, rushed to the site, where he learned that a certain tenant farmer was willing to sell a chunk "about the size of a water bucket." Bidding against another collector, the geologist succeeded in purchasing the piece for more than a hundred dollars in cash and departed with the prize in the back of his buggy. But upon learning that the tenant farmer did not actually own the field where the fragment had landed, the defeated bidder called the sheriff, and the argument ended in litigation. After several appeals, the Iowa supreme court ruled that a meteorite, although it might be classified as "celestial real estate," legally belongs to the owner of the land where it falls.

Ellis Hughes countered the case research of Oregon Iron and Steel's lawyers with a legal twist of his own. According to an Oregon statute, cultural relics belonged to the tribes who traditionally used them, but only for so long as such cultural use was sustained. Hughes argued that the meteorite was an abandoned Indian artifact, no longer in use, and therefore legally available to anyone who claimed it.

Hughes's defense team called on a seventy-year-old Klickitat man identified as Susap or Joseph. Tribal records from the early twentieth century show a Joseph Susap enrolled as a native of mixed heritage: Klickitat (a people with traditional territory north of the Columbia River) and Clackamas (a people whose traditional ground lay mostly south of the river). Susap testified that he remembered the meteorite from his childhood, when there were many trees around it. As a boy, he had often hunted in the company of a Clackamas headman named Wachino, who told Susap that the stone was made of iron, and that "young Clackamas warriors were initiated by being compelled on the darkest of nights to climb the hill and visit the lonely spot where the celestial visitor reposed." Tribal members would also go to this stone to wash their faces in the water that collected in the holes on its surface. Before hunts or raids, some would dip their bows and arrows in those natural basins. Susap said that Wachino and the old people called the stone Tomanowos. According to early anthropologist and linguist George Gibbs's *Dictionary of the Chinook Jargon*, "Ta-mah-no-us" was "a sort of guardian or familiar spirit; magic; luck; fortune."

For its second witness, Hughes's defense called Sol Clark, a forty-seven-year-old member of the Wasco tribe (a group whose traditional territory lay farther upstream on the Columbia River). Clark testified that he had heard about Clackamas medicine men performing rituals around Tomanowos, but thought that the practice had ceased around 1870, as tribal numbers began to dwindle in the face of encroaching white settlement.

Hughes's cultural argument seemed logical to several reporters on the scene, but it failed to sway the jury, which on April 27, 1904, decided in favor of Oregon Iron and Steel.

> The court found for the land owners and established a precedent that whatever falls from Mars, the moon, or any other distant sphere, whose occupants are not on visiting terms with the people on Earth, becomes a part of the hereditaments of the land on which it may fall. No syndicate from any of the planets having put in a claim for the meteorite, it is now recognized as the property of the owners of the land upon which it was found.

The court valued the meteorite at $150 and gave the company's owners permission to repossess the stone. Although Ellis Hughes filed an appeal, his claim seemed to be on its final tack. "If the plaintiff (Oregon Iron and Steel) wins out in suit," reported one paper, "the meteor will be added to the collections at the Portland Museum."

Then in January 1905, a new lawsuit appeared to further muddy the waters. Two local officials claimed that the meteorite had been stolen not from Oregon Iron and Steel property but from a contiguous parcel they jointly owned, and they pointed to a crater there to prove it. For the court's pleasure, they produced several witnesses who swore that the stone currently resting on Ellis Hughes's property had definitely emerged from the officials' land.

The jury, perhaps influenced by evidence that this second crater had been recently created with dynamite, again ruled for Oregon Iron and Steel. In addition, they re-valued the meteorite at a staggering $10,000. Suddenly, everyone from West Linn to the East Coast knew this stone represented something more than a curiosity. The judge placed the object under the protection of the Clackamas County sheriff pending the outcome of Hughes's appeal, which was still waiting to be scheduled before the state supreme court.

By now it was spring, and people were flocking to nearby Portland for the centennial celebration of the Lewis and Clark Expedition. As a show of good will, Ellis Hughes and Oregon Iron and Steel mutually agreed that the disputed stone could be carted to Oregon City and displayed on the courthouse square. Local boosters dared to hope that the many visitors drawn "to see the big meteorite will spend thousands of dollars here and the business men will reap the benefit."

The tourist attraction had hardly begun its journey to the courthouse square, however, when a state judge ruled that it must stop immediately. Its progress was halted next to a farm belonging to the Johnson family. In later years Harold Johnson, then a young boy, recalled with pride how his father was dep-utized to guard the stone, and how over the next few months his sleep was often interrupted by souvenir hunters who would sneak onto the property, hammers in hand, and attempt to crack off pieces. "The meteorite would ring like a bell when struck," Johnson remembered. "Often in the middle of the night the 'bell' would clang. Then out of bed jumped Father, grabbed his gun, and muttering to himself, rushed outside." Young Harold ended up with his own small chunk of the meteorite, obtained, he insisted, from a thief his dad had caught in the act.

It was July before the Oregon Supreme Court heard Hughes's appeal and upheld the circuit court's verdict in favor of Oregon Iron and Steel. In his decision, Justice C. J. Wolverton accepted the testimonies that tribal people had used the stone and its "kettle-holes" for spiritual purposes but stated that "mere evidence of a tradition that Indians reverenced a meteorite" was not enough to prove that they had legally taken possession of it, not even by moving the stone or fashioning the basins where they washed. "What is there to show that the Indians dug it from the earth and erected it in place, except its posture, or that they carved out the holes in its crown, except that they are there? If the first peoples never moved or altered the rock, how could they abandon it?" Wolverton concluded that he would follow the precedent set by the case of the Iowa aerolite, granting possession to the landowner.

With this final judgment in hand, Ellis Hughes had to admit defeat. The Clackamas County sheriff released custody of the meteorite to Oregon Iron and Steel, and the company hired twelve men and two teams of draft horses to transport their prize. Working night and day, the crews nudged a heavy-laden sledge to the mouth of the Tualatin River and onto a scow. A steamer towed the barge through the Willamette Falls Locks and down the Willamette River to Portland, where it was unloaded, dragged to a railroad scale, and certified at a weight of 31,107 pounds.

On August 23, 1905, the Willamette Meteorite was unveiled inside the Mining Building at the great Lewis and Clark Exposition. No less a dignitary than the director of the US Geological Survey pulled the cord that swept away an American flag covering the celebrated stone. That ceremony was followed by learned discourses from a US senator and a representative of the Boston Institute of Technology. While the scientist compared the shape of the mass to a flattened Liberty Bell, one reporter was struck by its resemblance to a crawling turtle. Predictably, the day's events led to fevered announcements concerning plans for a permanent display, with both Oregon City and Colonel Hawkins's Portland museum contending for the prize.

But before a winner could be determined, a third bidder emerged. Just as civic-minded locals had feared, the interloper was from out of town. New York mining heiress and American Museum of Natural History patroness Mrs. William E. Dodge offered $20,600 for sole possession of the meteorite, with the stipulation that it be kept intact. Oregon Iron and Steel accepted without a murmur of hesitation, and as soon as the Lewis and Clark Exposition closed, the stone was loaded on a train bound for New York City. Transferred from flatcar to a sophisticated heavy-duty cart, the Willamette Meteorite was paraded past Central Park to the steps of the grand museum. There, as local dignitaries swarmed aboard for a photo opportunity, one wheel of the cart sank deep into the asphalt street.

Backwash

Upon its arrival in New York, the Willamette Meteorite received a flurry of scientific attention. In the October 1905 issue of the *American Geologist*, Horace V. Winchell, the Minnesota collector who had secured the Iowa aerolite, took exception to many of the conclusions Henry Ward had reached while wallowing in the Oregon mud, especially his notion that rainwater could have eroded the fantastic pattern on the missile's trailing side. An expert from the American Museum of Natural History weighed in the following summer. There could be no doubt that the New York museum had cornered the market on spectacular aerolites, and that Mrs. Dodge's purchase ranked very high as a public attraction because of its aerodynamic cone, spectacularly corroded base, and dramatic backstory. Ellis Hughes's imaginative heist remained part of the appeal. The author attempted to clarify anomalies present in the texture and internal structure of the prize, comparing it to others held in the museum's meteorite collection.

In 1936, the pride of West Linn, along with 569 other specimens collected from around the globe, was moved to a grand display at the new Hayden Planetarium. There the Willamette Meteorite stood tall, second in size only to Robert Peary's Cape York Ahnighito.

The great Hall of Meteorites generated a new wave of publicity for the Willamette find and, perhaps, a small ripple of guilt from Dr. Clyde Fisher, chief curator of the New York museum. In 1938, Fisher mailed a package to Professor J. H. Pruett of the University of Oregon, who served as the western director for the American Meteorological Society and had worked tirelessly to support the study of Oregon meteorites. "I have had a small piece cut from the Willamette meteorite for the University of Oregon," Dr. Fisher wrote to Pruett. "We had the specimen polished and etched. . . . The weight of the specimen is now 181.1 grams. In sending this fragment of the Willamette Meteorite I do not want the University of Oregon to feel any definite obligation. I felt that your University should have a piece of the largest meteorite ever found in the United States since it came from your state."

Professor Pruett, in an attempt to assuage the feelings of scientifically-minded Oregonians, displayed the etched meteorite slice from the American Museum of Natural History alongside one of the rough fragments that had been hammered off on the Harold Johnson property. For good measure, Pruett commissioned a life-sized plaster model of the Willamette

Meteorite that for years stood on the porch of the university's chemistry building.

The receipt of this fragment also apparently spurred Pruett to send a photographer and journalism student to West Linn to look up Ellis Hughes. After the final state supreme court decision, he had returned to farming, but he had to admit that he remained bitter about his "inglorious and unjust defeat" three decades earlier.

The Guardian

The saga of the Willamette meteorite continued to evolve in the face of new scientific techniques and old-fashioned detective work. Sleuths who visited the stone's original depression near West Linn found that the pit was lined with a shard of oxidized iron crust, heavy with nickel; chemists determined that when the meteorite originally landed, it probably weighed over twenty tons. Modern laboratories also confirmed Henry Ward's notion that the stone's kettle holes had resulted from terrestrial weathering—when western Oregon's heavy annual rainfall and acidic forest environment met the meteorite's troilite mineral in what began as shallow depressions, the result was dilute, aerated sulfuric acid. Further activated by pulses of precipitation, over a long period of time these acidic puddles ate their way into the body of the stone.

The molecular structure of the Willamette Meteorite told a more complex story. This study required carefully polishing and etching small samples of the rock with acid, but luckily, there seemed to be plenty of those available. Today, the locations of museums around the world that claim a shard of the Willamette Meteorite range from Budapest to the Vatican, with many more fragments believed to be in private hands. Spectrographs and photochronographs of thin sections cut from miscellaneous shards reveal recrystallized kamacite and distorted, shock-melted troilite. Sensitive chemical analysis betrays varying percentages of nitrogen and phosphorous. Gas detectors sniff traces of helium, argon, and neon.

Although scientists would like to make a more comprehensive study of the original meteorite, Mrs. Dodge's stipulation that it remain intact, as a museum display, precludes any invasive sampling. Even so, geochemists and structural geologists have assembled a rough biography of the Willamette Meteorite that winds through at least five distinct stages. It is a story that continues to be modified as new evidence and new lab techniques appear.

The first chapter of the celestial stone's existence was set in outer space, and consisted of a primary slow-cooling period. This would correspond to clouds of matter cooling into the original planets of our solar system, in a time frame often estimated as four billion years ago.

At some point while still embedded in deep time, the meteorite's crystalline structure recorded a terrific shock and subsequent reheating. After that episode, it cooled again into a very different form. Other meteorites that have been analyzed show a similar pattern, and some scientists interpret this as an event similar to the catastrophic collision that created the asteroid belt between Mars and Jupiter.

Stage three was marked by a second, lesser shock—perhaps a glancing blow from another space object that flung the Willamette fragment out of a stable orbit into a more eccentric path that eventually brought it within range of Earth's gravitational pull. The associated annealing of this event left a new chemical fingerprint on its internal structure.

The fourth leg of its journey occurred when the meteor penetrated our atmosphere and fell to Earth in a fiery arc. This descent sculpted the classic dome shape, surface features, and unique boreholes.

Finally, long-term exposure to the earth's elements eroded the porous complex of basins and bowls into the rock. It is possible that the distinct shape of its troilite filaments, shocked and annealed in two separate incidents, contributed to this pattern.

While the meteor's tenure in space acquired ever more detailed interpretations, the earthly chapters of its story remained stuck on a slope above the Tualatin River. From the beginning of the Ellis Hughes saga, there had been speculation that the iron mass might have been transported to the Oregon woodlot during the glacial period. At the conclusion of his 1905 decision denying Hughes's final appeal, Judge Wolverton had veered from the legal to the geological: "The whole mass being corroded, rusty, and moss-grown," he reflected, combined with "the fact that granite boulders were lying in proximity to where it was found, would indicate that it might have been deposited there through the instrumentality of an ice floe." Three years later, geologist W. Hampton Smith, who had studied glacial erratics at the mouth of the Columbia River, expressed a similar viewpoint in a letter to the *Oregonian*. The Willamette Meteorite "did not fall where found," Smith insisted. "It is a glacial drift, and there dropped with drift not at all belonging to this region of the country. . . . Where or when it fell is not known as to time, but certainly prior to our last glacial period."

Sixty-seven years later, in 1975, the standard reference book for world meteorites, which covered a raft of subtleties exposed in recent geochemical and molecular studies, dismissed any idea that Ellis Hughes's stone might not have come to Earth near the hamlet of Willamette with one terse sentence: "The many suggestions that the meteorite had been moved from a different place appear to be unfounded."

Yet as some previous investigators had noted, the hollowed pit in the soft ground of the Willamette forest did not correlate with the craters made by other large meteorites upon impact. In 1986, Portland high school science teacher Richard Pugh revisited the shallow depression near West Linn where Ellis Hughes had first noticed the meteorite. There he picked up a light-colored twelve-inch boulder of granitic origin. Recalling Hughes's "white rock," Pugh searched through the poison oak that had grown up in the depression and found many similar pebbles of granodiorite, which does not occur in the bedrock of the Willamette Valley. Pugh postulated that the Willamette Meteorite originally plunged to Earth in southeastern British Columbia or northwestern Montana millions of years ago. During the most recent glacial epoch, less than a hundred thousand years ago, a lobe of advancing ice captured the meteorite. The stone, which had hurtled through space for so achingly long, then began a new journey, moving only a few inches a year, encased in ice alongside white granites of earthly origin.

The pace would pick up again, however. During the last ice age, the meteorite's icy crypt was caught up in one of the Lake Missoula floods that surged downstream across the Columbia Basin. The berg remained large enough to support the meteorite as the torrent turned the corner at Wallula Gap and squeezed through the Columbia River Gorge. Riding with the portion of the floodwaters that branched south into the Willamette Valley, the ice floe and its cargo finally came to rest in a back eddy near the mouth of the Tualatin River, surrounded by other flood erratics dropped along the flood's high-water mark in the Willamette hills, around 380 feet above sea level.

Back in New York in the late 1990s, the Willamette Meteorite was on the move yet again, to a position as the centerpiece of the American Museum of Natural History's new Cullman Hall of the Universe. At about the same time, the Confederated Tribes of Grand Ronde—a consortium of native peoples assembled from several displaced Columbia River Gorge and Coastal tribes who had been pushed into the Willamette Valley by white settlers—carried the depositions that Joseph Susap and Sol Clark made at Ellis Hughes's original trial to New York City as part of a new effort to restore the meteorite to Oregon. The Native American Graves Protection and Repatriation Act forced the museum to take their claims seriously, and an agreement was forged.

Through the permission of the Grand Ronde people, the Willamette Meteorite is to remain at the American Museum of Natural History as long as the tribe has access to it for cultural and religious purposes. The museum also created an internship for any Native American youth who comes to New York to study the institution's extensive collections of tribal artifacts.

Ellis Hughes did not live long enough to see his legal argument based upon tribal relics bear fruit. Nor did he ever reap any profit from the meteorite, beyond the quarters he collected at his viewing shed during a few months in 1903. But among his contemporaries, there were many who felt he had performed a great public service by dragging the Willamette Meteorite out of the forest. In the words of Northwest geologist W. Hampton Smith:

Science owes a debt of gratitude to the discoverer, Mr. Hughes. He erred in thinking that the meteor was his by right of discovery, and laboriously took it from the ground on which it was found to his own home. Had he not accidentally discovered it, however, it might have never been known. . . . I am informed that he has never been rewarded for his discovery and all the work he put upon it. From my point of view that is wrong. It is perhaps the most interesting sample of metal that ever came to earth from the starry depths that has been recovered. . . . It should have been kept here.

As a final stipulation of the agreement between the Confederated Tribes of the Grande Ronde and the American Museum of Natural History, if the Willamette Meteorite is ever retired from public display, its ownership will revert to the tribes. It is possible, therefore, that at some future date the turtle-shaped stone will once more journey across space and time, echoing one brief chapter of its long life history. If it should travel by rail, it will retrace its climactic Ice Age voyage across Lake Pend Oreille, through Spokane, and down the Columbia as it makes one more partial orbit of our small planet.

IV
A Taste for Roots

Bread for Hungry Mouths

Viewed from the scablands of southeastern Washington and northeastern Oregon, the Blue Mountains float like cumulus clouds above the eastern edge of the Columbia Basin. The Blues are old geologically; their terrain stretches more than sixty miles across the adjacent state corners, and their peaks rise over five thousand feet above the Snake and Columbia Rivers that circle below them. Early white travelers described the plains that border these waterways as stark and thirsty places, and looked to the shimmering bluish heights above for comfort.

The fingered ridges that work their way downslope from the high country are treeless along their tops and do not appear to offer much promise of water. Yet as the snow recedes each spring, life-giving moisture oozes from every crack of their broken knuckles. An April traveler hungry for early wildflowers can wander up a digit, such as Biscuit Ridge, and enjoy sagebrush buttercup, blue-eyed Mary, yellowbell, spring beauty, shooting star, ballhead waterleaf, and long-flowered bluebell just by stepping a few yards.

Although such showy flowers are plentiful, the real abundance appears on slumping roadcuts and within bony swales, where yellow flowers with distinctive dark-green leaves blanket the muddy basalt. These are members of a diverse genus that we call by two common names: biscuitroot, after a bread-like staple that many western tribes prepare from the roots, and desert parsley, after their habitat and finely cut leaves. The genus name *Lomatium*, from the Latin "winged seed," refers to the severely flattened edges of their ovoid seeds. Several species carry seductive strong aromas that have been compared to cultivated parsley-family relatives such as anise, fennel, or caraway.

From my vantage point on Biscuit Ridge, these modest plants seem as common as the gravels that trickle downhill. Above each clump of lacy leaves, a single reddish stem rises no higher than my boot top. A compound flower head composed of a dozen dense florets rides atop the stem like a small yellow umbrella. This shape supplied the original family name Umbelliferae (now changed to Apiaceae) and remains the common calling card of the tribe.

My field guide confirms my guess that this cheery yellow biscuitroot is the one known as cous, pronounced both as "coos" and "cows." Many people—especially members of several Plateau tribes who gather these biscuitroots for food—will quickly praise their flavor, whether boiled, roasted, or pounded and formed into cakes.

The crew of Lewis and Clark's Corps of Discovery had their first taste of cous in late fall of 1805 at the Cascades of the Columbia, near modern Bonneville Dam. Here William Clark watched a broad array of native bands trading robes, skins, bear-grass, camas roots, and some flat cakes that he and Lewis called "cha-pel-el" or "shapalell." It's not too hard to find corollaries for their spellings in the Chinookan word *a-sáblal* and the Chinook jargon, *saplíl*, both of which translate as "bread."

Although the captains described trading for "a kind of biscuit" during their winter at the mouth of the Columbia, the shapalell did not assume its full importance in their diet until their return journey upstream in 1806. After arriving back at the Cascades of the Columbia in early April, Lewis again noted a lively traffic in goods, with the root bread as one stock item among many. On April 12, he purchased "2 pieces of Chapellel and Some roots"; two days later, approaching the Dalles, his grocery list included five dogs, along with hazelnuts, dried berries, and more root bread.

As the Corps continued upriver, Meriwether Lewis made a connection between shapalell and the abundant yellow flowers that he was seeing along the way. His naturalist's eye recognized them as members of the same family as carrots and dill, familiar from eastern gardens. Near the mouth of the Walla Walla River, he pressed a sample and attached a brief label: "An umbelliferous plant of the root of which the Wallowallas make a kind of bread. The natives call it shappalell." He tried to approximate the Sahaptin word for the root, *xáws*, which he rendered as "cous" and sometimes "cows." Lewis's designation was later married to the Latin genus to arrive at the scientific name of *Lomatium cous*.

During the month of May, while making final preparations for crossing the Continental Divide, the Corps camped on the Clearwater River above its confluence with the Snake, near the village of a hospitable Nez Perce leader called Broken Arm. There they found spring food processing in full swing. "The noise of their women pounding roots reminds me of a nail factory," Lewis remarked. "The Indians seem well pleased, and I am confident that they are not more so than our men who have their stomachs once more well filled with horsebeef and mush of the bread of cows." In other words, the men were getting plenty of horse meat and cous bread to eat. Lewis's use of the letter "w" instead of "u" in his spelling of cous can sometimes be confusing, but his description of the tuber that was providing so much of the Corps' sustenance is filled with important details.

He compared cous to the ginseng he had grown up with back in Virginia and the baked camas bulbs that hospitable tribes had fed to the white visitors from the moment they arrived in the Columbia drainage. Lewis not only paid close attention to cooking and preservation methods that might benefit the Corps, but he also caught a hint of the seasonal rounds involved in collecting and processing the resource.

> The cows is a knobbed root of an irregularly rounded form not unlike the Gensang in form and consistence. This root they collect, rub off a thin black rhind which covers it and pounding it expose it in cakes to the sun. these cakes are about an inch and ¼ thick and 6 by 18 in width, when dryed they either eat this brad [bread] alone without any further preperation, or boil it and make a thick muselage; the latter is most comin and much the most agreeable. The flavor

of this root is not very unlike the gensang. this
root they collect as early as the snows disappear
in the spring and continue to collect it until
the quawmash [camas] supplys it's place which
happens about the latter end of June.

As the Corps stockpiled food for its upcoming journey, the
great quantities of roots processed with mortar and pestle by Nez
Perce women became all the more evident. On May 19, a group
of his men returned from a trading session with "about 6 bushels
of the cows roots and a considerable quantity of bread of the
same materials."

Recalling their difficult mountain journey of the previous
fall, the Americans wanted still more. The captains debated
sending the crew out to dig on their own but thought better of
it. "We would make the men collect these roots themselves but
there are several species of hemlock which are so much like the
cows that it is difficult to discriminate them from the cows and
we are afraid that they might poison themselves," wrote Lewis.
He was wise to be cautious: the extremely toxic water hemlock,
Cicuta douglasii, is also a member of the parsley family, and it
does grow in that vicinity. Plateau plant identification is not an
easy learning curve for newcomers.

Choosing to rely on local knowledge, Lewis and Clark
issued an allowance of trade goods to the men so they could
each purchase "a parsel of roots and bread from the natives
as his stores for the rocky mountains." The visitors continued
to barter for more cous until early June, when they decided
they had enough to see them through the mountain pass. By
then, the Nez Perce women had switched their focus to digging
camas bulbs. These the Americans found much less palatable,

leading to disappointment with the tribe's departing gift. "The Broken Arm gave Capt. C. a few dryed Quawmas [camas] roots as a great present," wrote Lewis on their last day. "In our estimation those of cows are much better, I am confident they are much more healthy."

Salt and Pepper

On a recent cold morning in early March, botanist Pam Camp and I strolled along the western curl of the Columbia River's Big Bend. Behind us, the North Cascades remained fully wrapped in winter's grip, but in the lower country, the snow had melted away from the southern exposures. Ropes of freshly exposed gopher work glistened with frost, and although the first buttercups had yet to appear, we were hopeful that the seasonal biscuitroot clock had begun to tick. Camp's experienced eye landed on a short strand of green thread easing up from a crack in the rocky ground. A few steps farther along, more visible leaves branched upward, like tiny fingers reaching for the sun. We circled a pocket of shattered basalt where she spotted an umbrella, no larger than a thumbnail, made up of tiny white florets. I dropped to my knees to eye the dark purple anthers that bristled among the white petals—the inspiration for the flower's common name of salt and pepper.

Although most wildflower manuals equate salt and pepper with *Lomatium gormanii*, that would be far too simple. There are actually three different small, early flowering biscuitroot species in the Columbia country that feature white petals and purple anthers. All three also share many characteristics of leaf and stem. All three have edible roots, though not as large or as popular among tribal families as cous. All three spread across the Columbia's shrub-steppe habitats with subtle variations. All three may be found in association with others of their kin, and their identification can confound the most dedicated of plant lovers. Although a professional botanist, Pam Camp readily admits to struggling with these biscuitroots and is sympathetic to a layperson trying to navigate the taxonomic maze.

She directed my attention to the ground. I already knew that an inch or so below the earth's surface, the root of each salt and pepper forms a garbanzo bean–sized globe of almost perfect roundness. But I didn't know that the root of a closely related cousin does the same. In order to tell them apart, Camp explained, we were supposed to look for subtle differences in the tendrils that sprout from the bottom of the root, in the simplicity of the plant's growth form, and in other features that would not appear until later in the season, such as the pattern of the oil ducts of its mature fruits. And if we became frustrated, she added, we should keep in mind that some botanists insist these two species cannot be separated in the field—not so long ago, in fact, they were lumped together in the species *confusum.*

To further the confusion, there is a third species that bears an almost identical bite-sized tuber. But on its very bottom point, where its two close cousins sprout a few hair-like rootlets, this one extends a stringy root that swells into another tuber. If a plant is particularly robust, this root may continue to grow, sprouting several more distinct swellings, like beads on a delicate necklace buried ever deeper in the rocky soil. The Okanagan Salish word for this deceptive plant translates as "something tied up on the end"—a good name, if you can ever find the necklace's elusive final clasp.

Camp and I considered the challenge of teasing those extra beads out of the ground without breaking the connecting strands, for if they were lost on the first stab, we would misdiagnose the species. As we discerned more and more of the tiny white parasols peeking above the ground, we wondered if maybe this would be the year that each of us, in our own way, would circle around to some kind of understanding of the biscuitroots. Or at least of this early group of three, with anthers as purple as sea urchins.

Camp unfolded a pocketknife and set to work. I slid a sharpened hardwood stick between two rocks and wriggled it around, attempting to pry out a tuber that had sprouted between two stones. I thought I was making some progress when the stem snapped off just below ground level. After the same thing happened twice more, I began grubbing with my hands, easing stones out of the way until I finally levered a little round root up from below. Upon closer examination, I discovered what might be the nub of a single broken string on its bottom.

Perhaps a little impatient, I broke off several more roots and stems before realizing that I was fighting frozen clumps of soil. Fingers numbed, I looked up to find Camp in the same claw-handed situation. On this particular morning, we were not going to define any species of salt and pepper for certain. Defeated but exhilarated—a whole season of biscuitroot searches lay ahead— we trudged back up the frost-rimmed slope. "How can it be spring for them," Camp asked, "when it's still winter for us?"

Unsettled

The biscuitroots of the Columbia Plateau have been dealing with the challenging environment of their homeland for a very long time. They have adapted to the short and early growing season, the stiff winds, the cold winters, and the long summer droughts that have long limited vegetation across the region. The compact size of many species, such as the salt and peppers, enhances their ability to flower very soon after leafing out in the spring. Low growth habits and the lack of a central protruding stem protect the delicate leaves from buffeting winds, and keep them close to a relatively warm layer of air near the ground. Narrow leaf segments, often sliced to minute fineness, provide more surface area for photosynthesis in dry conditions. Multiple dense flower heads, with male and female flowers present on the same plant, allow for both outcrossing and self-pollination by insects or wind. The smaller species quickly complete their reproductive cycles before the rocky soils lose their moisture during the inevitable summer drought. Fruits mature rapidly into winged seeds that dry up and sail away on afternoon winds. Finely cut leaves and stout stems desiccate in a matter of days until they too disappear. Underground, many of these *Lomatiums* harbor tuberous roots in a wonderful variety of shapes and sizes. These tubers store nutritious carbohydrates during tough winter conditions, then send that essential energy aboveground in the spring to support flowering and seed production.

Because most *Lomatiums* come and go so quickly, any attempt to understand them must persist through many successive springs. A year after our first salt and pepper excursion, Pam Camp suggested that I travel to the heart of the Columbia Basin, along the base of Saddle Mountain's long spine. There, amidst an extensive talus slope that tumbled off the central ridge, I would find a most unusual species of biscuitroot. But if I wanted to see it in bloom, she suggested that I get going soon.

A pair of basalt knobs standing as sentinels directed me to the place easily enough. The massive rockfall they guarded looked dauntingly steep, with only an occasional clump of serviceberry or syringa to indicate that there might be any soil to anchor a small plant.

"They're living right in the rocks," Camp had told me. "And keep climbing—they'll be further upslope than you think."

The boulders at the bottom of the slope were refrigerator-sized, forcing me to keep my eyes squarely on my feet as I spider-walked uphill. The cracks between the big boulders penetrated many layers down. After hopping a hundred yards or more, I crossed a stream of smaller fist-sized rocks that rolled beneath every foothold. I moved on through a wilderness of scree that continued to slip in a slow-motion avalanche. I saw no green-ery at all within this constant motion until, only a few inches beyond one of my outstretched hands, a cluster of leaves mate-rialized, tatted into lacework so fine that they looked like fuzzy gray-green kitten paws against the dark basalt.

More of the paws appeared above and below me. Rocks obscured most of their flowers and stems, but I eventually found some purple blooms with yellow anthers—colors that mirrored the crusty lichens washing across the basalt walls on either side of the talus slope. Many of the blossoms were already aging into an even deeper purple, camouflaged as if they meant to sink into the dark shadows of the scree. This was obviously the strange new biscuitroot, Hoover's desert parsley (*Lomatium tuberosum*), that Pam Camp had sent me in search of.

The fact that any of these plants could keep their heads above the shifting rockslide long enough to send up flower-ing stems seemed like a miracle, and a look into some of the cracks revealed several kitten paws partially crushed beneath tumbled stones. Gently rolling away rocks, I teased out one swollen potato-shaped tuber, the obvious source for its Latin species name of "knobby." Its broken tip hinted at a much longer serpentine body that slithered deep into the hidden talus world. This severed portion would remain buried, safe within the turmoil, ready to send up leaves the next spring. Hoover's desert parsley has found a way to embrace the chaos around it by developing a specialized ability to retreat and survive. Whenever a shifting stone snaps off part of a root, both remnants have the ability to sprout new growth, doubling the chance of successful blooms in succeeding years.

It is tempting to wonder if Ice Age floodwaters somehow contributed to such deft adaptations. The succession of floods that crashed across the Columbia Basin would have carried innumerable seeds along with the soil that was swept away. Whenever the water slowed, an unpredictable mix of sand, silt, gravel, rocks, and ice-rafted boulders was deposited in its wake. Some of the seeds caught in this detritus would have sprouted, forming new colonies with curious blends of plant species, biscuitroots included.

Only a few miles upstream from my perch on the scree slope, one of those great floods had carved a gigantic amphitheater on a terrace several hundred feet above the Columbia. Its Sahaptin place name could be rendered in English as "Where the Waters Turned"—an apt description of a powerful agitating cycle that tore into cliff faces as it circled and slowed. The amphitheater's lower level is covered with gravels dropped by the floods and edged by blowing sand dunes. Not surprisingly, hosts of *Lomatiums* thrive across the rough bench.

Although those amphitheater biscuitroots, and the more specialized desert parsley that has burrowed into the scree slopes of Saddle Mountain, are living in habitats created by sudden floods, their lifespan has to be measured on an entirely different scale of time. Plant systematists who study *Lomatium* pollination leap back at least as far as the late Pliocene and visualize changes in millions, not thousands, of years. Geneticists trace plant ranges that flow like amoebas across a landscape, developing new species at their extremities. Geologic events might separate closely related clusters. Some of these colonies might survive in isolation, morph into a slightly different form, then be reunited with their ancestors by gradual changes in geology or climate. The movements of the Cordilleran glaciers and the spurt of apocalyptic floods that ended the Pleistocene represent only two of the challenges that these plants have weathered.

Within the Intermountain West, this restless clan includes about three dozen or so different species. For all their abundance, most of these biscuitroots live so inconspicuously that they have never acquired memorable common names. The fact that "cous" is sometimes applied to several different biscuitroots as a general term only adds to the confusion.

Pioneering naturalist David Douglas would have sympathized with this dilemma. When he traversed the northern Plateau in the early spring of 1826, he quickly collected five different kinds of biscuitroots, including two or three with white flowers and purple anthers. None of them had the kind of large, striking flowers that might sell to British gardeners, and none of them displayed any clearly defined characteristics that would allow for field identification on the fly. Douglas entered them in his notebook as Umbellifores and moved on. In the two centuries that have passed since, several taxonomists have devised keys to separate the *Lomatiums*, with words such as "variable" and "overlap" cropping up frequently in their technical descriptions. Field researchers not only continue to describe new species but also consistently manage to find plants that do not fit a prescribed pattern. This is why botanists refer to the genus as "unsettled," and why, to a novice, the *Lomatium* complex seems like a wheeling flock of migrant shorebirds that never quite settles to Earth.

As a professional, Pam Camp understands the value of rigorous scientific work, both in the lab and out in the field. Even with modern techniques, she believes it will take geneticists quite a while to sort out exactly what is going on with *Lomatiums*. "No single factor is going to solve the puzzle," she says. "You have to consider each plant and its makeup. You have to look at how and where it lives. You have to weigh everything else around it."

From my tenuous foothold about a quarter of the way up that Saddle Mountain talus slope, I tried to relate her words, and a single gray-green Hoover's desert parsley, to the larger world. It was more than I could manage.

The Rounds

Lomatiums have provided a key resource for the Plateau tribes with whom they have shared territory since the end of the last ice age. As late as the 1970s, families living around the Yakama Reservation described uses for no less than fourteen different species of biscuitroots. Although stems, leaves, and seeds all received some mentions, the majority involved the digging and processing of the roots for food.

Two of these tubers are clearly the most utilized: cous (*Lomatium cous*), the one that appears so often in Meriwether Lewis's journals, and Canby's biscuitroot (*Lomatium canbyi*), which he never mentions at all. These two biscuitroots are easy to tell apart. The flowers of *cous* are yellow; those of *canbyi* are white. *Cous* tubers vary wildly in shape, like a paper bag blown up and scrunched in every possible way. *Canbyi*, on the other hand, produces perfectly globular spheres that, aside from depressions caused by rocks or roots, could be mistaken for dirty golf balls. Cous dominates the southern half of the Plateau—southeastern Washington, eastern Oregon, and adjacent areas of western Idaho—while the range of Canby's biscuitroot extends from central Washington along a westward curve that follows the foothills of the Cascade Range south to the Columbia.

When Lewis and Clark entered that region on their return trip upstream along the Columbia in spring 1806, they found that their visit coincided with the season for digging biscuitroots. At Celilo Falls on April 17, they tried to trade for some packhorses to cross the mountain ranges ahead, but had no luck, because, Clark reported, "The chief informed me that their horses were all in the plains with their womin gathering roots." Plateau families, especially the women and children, were flowing across the countryside, branching and turning and joining again: season-dependent, flexible, persistent, hardy, resourceful, skilled, and knowledgeable to a degree that the white visitors could sense but in their short time on the scene could never quite grasp.

A little further upstream, at the confluence of the Palouse and Snake Rivers, Lewis and Clark might have seen the ancestors of Mary Jim setting out with twined root bags and digging sticks. In a 1980 oral account, Jim described her family's travel routes, which had persisted since the early nineteenth century, and for untold generations before that.

"I am a Palouse Indian from the Snake River, where my people have always lived. God put us there, and we prayed, thanking Him for the river and the salmon and all good things," Mary Jim began. "My father was Alliyua, Thomas Jim, and his father was Fishhook Jim, Chowatyet. We lived at village Tasawiks. My grandmother was Amtaloot, who was from Priest Rapids.

Grandmother taught me many things about how to live when I grew up."

A large part of Mary Jim's education consisted of learning the rounds for gathering roots—where and when her family sought cous and several different biscuitroots, as well as a variety of other tubers.

"We would start to move in March. We would move to Soap Lake, dig certain kinds of roots. They used to dig skúkul [Lomatium canbyi] and some other roots."

Mary Jim's uncle Harry Jim would lead the family to Colfax for still more variety. They also camped on the Waterville Plateau north and west of Soap Lake. From there, they would move up in elevation as the season progressed, arriving on sites at the most favorable moment for gathering certain species. They worked "all over that big hill, Badger Mountain," Mary Jim said. "We used to stay there. That's where people used to gather, play stick games, dance the Washat, you know, the Seven Drum Religion. We used to race horses at Badger Mountain.

"When we were done there, we moved back to Snake River, last of May maybe, and then salmon came up the river. In the fall, we went over to Walla Walla to dig cous. That's where we used to camp and dig.

"Then we went up into the mountains to dig other kinds of roots. You baked some of them. We traveled a lot. You ought to have seen them horses: packin', packin', packin'."

Mary Jim's relatives, who were affiliated with Palouse, Wanapum, Yakama, and other tribal entities, spoke different Sahaptin tongues. Their names for the roots that fed them varied with place, time, growth stage, preparation technique, and taste. Mary Jim learned these names and places from her grandmother and uncle, who had been going to their special sites since they were small children, absorbing the knowledge of generations and passing it along.

For people across the northern part of the Plateau—central and northeastern Washington, the Idaho panhandle, and southeastern British Columbia—the white-flowered Canby's biscuitroot is more accessible than its southern cousin, cous. Elders of the Spokane tribe tell a story that explains how these plants are distributed across their corner of the Columbia Basin. A character they called Doodlebug had just spent a day fishing and decided to conceal a nice salmon he had speared from his hardworking sister, who had spent her day busily digging roots of several kinds. Upon discovering Doodlebug's deception, Little Sister was so filled with anger that she clambered up a ridge above the Spokane River with all her roots and walked to the edge of the cliff. There, to spite her deceitful brother, she scattered those roots to the four cardinal directions. The roots flew away to new places—including some especially fine p'úxʷpuxʷ that landed on Ice Age flood-scoured grounds to the south and west, where people still dig them today. The Spokane word for Canby's biscuitroot is p'úxʷpuxʷ, and when native speakers pronounce it, their mouths and cheeks round out to form perfect globes, just like the roots.

Spokane tribal member Ann McCrae smiled when she spoke to me about a previous generation of women going out to dig. "My mom and her cronies," she said. "That's what I called them. She had friends from up on the Colville Reservation and a couple from around here, and they would get in the car and drive all over the place. After they got old, I was often the one who drove them around, to all their different family digging places, and to others that they had heard about. They would talk and laugh and point this way and that, and tell me to keep on going. One time we drove down to Walla Walla for cous and just kept on going all the way to Las Vegas. They thought that was really funny.

"But they were respectful at the same time. There was this rock they always talked about somewhere near Coffeepot Lake, and it led to several good places to dig $p'\acute{u}x^w\,pux^w$. They said the steep side of the rock was all fluted with grooves that swooped down just like the hair on the back of a woman's head. They would go visit that rock, then go dig roots. On their way home, they would stop again to leave a few of the best roots beside the rock. They said everybody did that. Whenever you went by, you would see offerings of roots spread out at its base, as a way of saying thanks."

Feasts

In the spring of 1822, Hudson's Bay Company clerk Finan McDonald kept the journal for the Spokane House trading post, just downstream from the present-day city of Spokane. During early April, he reported that tribal groups from a dozen or more Salish bands were gathered along the river for runs of steelhead and trout, but as the month wore on, the people began to slip away.

> April 26th . . . fine mild weather A few Indians tented off to go and collect roots . . .
> Sunday 28th . . . A party of Indians removed off some to gather roots and a few to go in search of beaver . . .
> Monday 29th . . . A few Indians removed off toward the plains to gather roots . . .

These bands were heading for the open country of the Columbia Basin. In certain areas, such as the vicinity of Soap Lake or Badger Mountain, they would have crossed paths with Sahaptin families. Then, relationships would naturally overlap, creating a web of kinship and plant knowledge that would overwhelm the information any binomial Latin designation could provide. Their complex annual rounds, which considered factors as minute as snowpack in a side canyon or the taste preferences of a distant cousin, never took exactly the same shape twice.

When Lewis and Clark encountered people gathering food near the mouth of the Klickitat River in April 1806, they paused to add a new plant to their collection. The specimen in their herbarium is clearly barestem biscuitroot (*Lomatium nudicaule*), for which they noted a tribal use: "The natives eat the tops & boil it Sometimes with their Soup . . . the same as we use celery."

That comparison still seems prescient. Today, in the back-and-forth way of cultures sharing place, tribes across the Plateau call the food that anchors their first spring feasts "Indian celery." There are several different species that answer to this description, and women carefully pick the earliest tender shoots before any flowers appear to serve with early roots, such as cous.

David Douglas experienced that kind of spring bounty around the mouth of the Okanogan River when, just as the snow was receding, he collected an "*Umbelliferae*, perennial; flowers purple; one of the strongest of the tribe found in the upper country; the tender shoots are eaten by the natives." This was fernleaf biscuitroot (*Lomatium dissectum*), a very robust plant often called "chocolate tips" because of its brownish-purple flower heads. Other Plateau people get their initial dose of fresh spring vitamins from Gray's desert parsley (*Lomatium grayi*), clipping the young stems just as they emerge from the ground. The strong taste of this Indian celery outstrips that of fennel or Italian parsley, providing a bite clearly distinct from other shoots that share the "celery" name.

For First Feast, people gather fresh shoots of certain plants that form part of their cultural traditions. At the same time, they dig particular early roots and prepare them according to their family ways. Much more than a meal, First Feast is a ceremony renewing a sacred compact, and various Plateau creation stories teach the same lesson in different ways: back in the earliest times, the roots promised to take care of the people, as long as the people promised to take care of the roots.

That ancient pact is evident in late April of each year in the Spokane country, when students from the school on the Spokane Reservation join people of all ages on one communal harvest day at a traditional site on the flood-scoured scablands to dig p'úxʷ puxʷ and other roots. Everyone arrives carrying their favorite digging sticks and root bags. Elders offer prayers to begin the work. Clumps of children gather around to learn the skill of starting their stick at a good distance from their target; of twisting the handle so its recurved end will loosen the dirt and rocks; of levering the stick down and cupping their hand beneath its point to lift a root out of the ground.

As the crowd sifts through the sagebrush, fanning out across low escarpments of worn basalt, three small girls arrange phlox and prairie rocket into a lovely pink bouquet. Lark, sage, and vesper sparrows hop up on bunchgrass tussocks to sing out territory. Harvester ants carry seeds across bare sand and disappear into their small conical mounds. A horned lizard puffs up beneath the shadow of a second grader's hand. Another student helps his mother with a particularly stubborn biscuitroot that seems to be intertwined with the root system of an ancient sagebrush. "This bush," whispers the mother to her son, as he leans on the stick for all he is worth, "does not want to share with us."

Experienced kids carry their first roots to a circle of elders seated in folding chairs, hold them in front of a favorite auntie, then drop them into a five-gallon plastic bucket. The seated elders talk and laugh as they lean forward to pick the roots from the bucket one by one. Quick fingers strip away a blackish layer of skin, revealing firm white biscuitroot flesh. A strange but irresistible odor, similar to turpentine or kerosene, emanates from the roots.

Back home, the roots will be strung into necklaces for drying as winter food. Many liken them to popcorn, and say the longer the *p'ux*^{w} *pux*^{w} dries, the better it tastes. They look forward to days when they can snack on the strung roots, each bite recalling the crisp delights of spring in the open country.

By tracking the progress of different sites through the spring, families time their rounds of digging to the period of maximum nutritional value. They also, by design, take steps to make sure the cycle will continue. Parts of roots broken off by sharp digging sticks remain healthy and stimulated underground, like garden bulbs that flourish when divided. Diggers also turn maturing seed tops back into the ground, giving individual seeds a chance to sprout with a little extra protection.

In much the same way that recipes for roots vary from family to family, the nature of the plants themselves seems to change from one edge of their range to the other. At traditional digging sites along the Columbia's Big Bend, the skin of the *canbyi* tubers takes on a slightly different color and texture, and the roots emit less of that distinct kerosene smell that fills the air around the Spokane grounds. Botanists insist that such plants all across the Columbia Basin belong to the same *canbyi* species, but Sahaptin speakers call the variety from the Big Bend by a different name and say that its taste is rougher. They sort them into different bags and use different methods of preparation.

While walking on a stony ridgetop near Saddle Mountain, I listened to a Sahaptin man describe how he used to watch his mother and aunties dry, bake, roast, grind, and boil different species of biscuitroots in different sequences to achieve the result they wanted. The ladies would keep all their roots separated until each one was prepared, and then they would combine the array to make small cakes or cookies—a handful of this and a handful of that, shaped into edible form by slapping the palms together. The parents lured their children to participate with the promise that they could keep any cookies they made. Each handful had a distinctive taste, and each combination went together in a particular way. You learned how to make what you liked. After patting together their cookies, the kids laid them in the sun, then turned them carefully until they were dry enough to store.

One group of neighbors, who gathered roots in many of the same places as the family that made cookies, formed its pounded roots into something more like large pancakes. Each round would be about an inch thick and more than a foot across. The dad would bend together a willow frame, then build a low, slow-burning fire inside. The family laid its pancakes on top of the frame, so that the fire's smoke could slowly cure them. Different method. Different taste.

The Sahaptin man arched his fingers to imitate how that red willow frame allowed the smoke to curl around each giant flatbread and seal in all the flavor. He made it easy to picture

Lewis and Clark breathing in that same delicious smell, then trying to barter for one more round of shapallel bread.

Three decades after Lewis and Clark packed their shapallel on the Clearwater River, the Reverend Henry Spalding came to the same area as a Protestant missionary to the Nez Perce. He was interested in the natural history of the region and, in the early 1840s, Harvard botanist Asa Gray suggested that Spalding collect plants in his new domain. The reverend took up the challenge with vigor, often setting out on collecting ventures with tribal guides. After one such excursion, Spalding pressed the leaves and flowers of a biscuitroot; he sliced its spherical root into a marshmallow shape with a sharp knife and glued one flat side to his paper. He made a special inscription to annotate his work: THIS IS THE REAL INDIAN COUS. What he appears to have collected, however, is not *Lomatium cous*, with its bag-like tuber, but rather a fine example of the round-rooted *Lomatium canbyi*.

As I stood in the stacks of the Gray Herbarium, looking at the yellowed specimen paper that the Reverend Spalding had labeled with such confidence, it seemed like an appropriate biscuitroot trick. One way or another, they were going to have the last laugh.

V

A POSSIBLE FRIEND

The Go-Between

During the last two decades of the nineteenth century, multiple discoveries of precious metals—from silver in the Coeur d'Alene Mountains to lead-zinc on the lower Pend Oreille River, from gold on the upper Columbia River to copper above the Colville Valley—transformed the character of the Inland Northwest. Young men of all descriptions rushed to the region to seek their main chance.

William Morley Manning's story began like many of them. A farmer's son wandering far from his home in rural Ontario, the twenty-year-old Manning was first attracted to the gold strikes around Idaho's Salmon River. He apparently liked what he found there, for in 1897 he filed a Declaration of Intent to become a US citizen. Within the next year, he returned to eastern Canada to study mining engineering at the Ontario School of Practical Science in Toronto.

He soon made his way west again. In October 1899, the Northwest Mining Association held an industrial exposition during its annual gathering in Spokane, the main supply center for the mining industries of the entire Inland Northwest. William Manning was in charge of a large display from southeastern British Columbia's Ymir district near Nelson, touting the area's potential in an attempt to attract investors.

January of 1900 found him traveling in northeast Washington in the company of a millionaire mine owner who was planning to develop a gold claim in the area. That year's Washington census lists Manning as an assayer living near the town of Bossburg in Stevens County, which at that time covered the entire northeast corner of the state and encompassed several rich mining districts. By August, according to the *Bossburg Journal*, he was in charge of thirty employees at the new First Thought Mine, located on a hill above the Kettle River. In his spare time, he was busily locating and filing mining claims on adjoining properties, both in his own name and in partnership with one of the trustees of the First Thought.

As development of that operation continued apace, Manning visited the superintendent of the Colville Indian Agency in company with Alex Herrin, an enrolled tribal member who owned an allotment adjacent to the mine. Herrin was seeking approval from the superintendent to lease part of his allotment to the mining company for a tramway that would ferry wood and supplies to the mine. Manning had offered Herrin $150 for the right-of-way, and the superintendent saw no problem with the arrangement.

Between 1900 and 1905, Manning worked as the superintendent of three mines in the area as the fortunes of various enterprises waxed and waned. He became well-known in the nearby towns of Bossburg and Orient, whose newspaper editors considered his comings and goings worth frequent mention in their "Local Briefs" columns. In summer 1903, the *Kettle River Journal* shared a newsworthy item:

> Billie Manning's reputation as a "high flyer"
> was emphasized the other day. He flew over the
> head of a cayuse, and the contact between his
> head and a metamorphic formation assayed only
> a trace.

At some point during these high-flying years, Manning developed an interest in the tribes of the surrounding area. He became acquainted with Chief Joseph—the headman of the associated nontreaty Nez Perce bands who had startled the nation in 1877 with their attempt to escape placement on a reservation. Joseph's painful journey since that time had landed his cadre on the Colville Reservation, among a mix of northern Plateau peoples who did not share the Nez Perce culture or language. The chief would have been just over sixty years old when he met Manning, who had been born the same year as the Nez Perce's long march. The miner and the chief apparently established a rapport, for at some time before he passed away in 1904, Joseph presented Manning with a council pipe

> . . . of serpentine rock having a solid silver inlay
> from end to end. . . . It is about 12" long, one
> and a half at large end by three quarters at small
> end and weighs about a couple of pounds. This

pipe was a personal gift from Chief Joseph and is contained in a leather case which is beaded to represent the design on the pipe which is the spear and fish of plenty.

Manning also obtained at least two other artifacts belonging to Joseph. One was a foot-tall woven basket with a body of dark willow roots. A geometric design fashioned from light-colored cedar roots formed the wrap. The weaver finished the piece with buckskin strings around the top and a shoulder strap for ease of carrying.

A second item, which Manning described as a "Joseph war bonnet," was made of eagle feathers tipped with red-dyed smaller feathers. It was bound with mane and tail horsehair dyed in greens and reds, then set into a beaver-skin headpiece. The bonnet could be tied with a pair of long strings cut from ermine fur. Joseph had several war bonnets, and Manning possibly acquired his from one of Joseph's nephews, to whom they were bequeathed at the chief's funeral potlatch.

In his tabulation of these artifacts, written two decades after their acquisition, Manning related nothing about how he first met Joseph, or what price he paid for any of the pieces, or what he might have done to deserve the council pipe gift. Yet such exchanges would not have been considered unusual at the time. Chief Joseph was a well-known figure, respected by many in the white community. Plenty of collectors recognized the cultural value and craftsmanship inherent in tribal artifacts, and it was understood that many tribal people made and sold them as a source of income. Perhaps of greater significance was the fact that a clear majority of anthropologists, government officials, and white settlers of that era believed that

Native American people faced inevitable extinction, so to the collectors, it only made sense to purchase such curios before their source disappeared. After Joseph's death, headdresses and articles of clothing that were reputed to have belonged to the famous Nez Perce chief went on display in towns throughout the Inland Northwest.

In time, Manning purchased a variety of other pieces from people on the Colville Reservation. Some, such as a pair of "men's buckskin gloves with gauntlet," heavily beaded with a floral pattern and fringed along the gauntlet's outside edge, represent typical fine bead- and hidework of the time, and may well have been made with a purchaser like Manning in mind. Others, such as a selection of well-used fishing gear collected around Kettle Falls, serve as historic confirmation of timeless knowledge.

The most spectacular of these is a double-headed fish spear originally hafted on a sixteen-foot cedar shaft. The working end consists of two slender hardwood tines almost three feet long, joined at one end to form a crotch and held apart at the other end by a wooden spreader. Nooses of closely woven native hemp cord are secured midway down each tine, just above the spreader. The twin lines, both about two feet long, flutter off the tines and are attached to sharp iron spearpoints. The bases of these barbs are carefully cupped so that they nestle onto the blunt tine ends like ball-and-socket joints. Pine pitch was used to glue the spearpoints firmly in place. When this spear was cast and struck a large Chinook salmon, the points would work loose so that the full power of the fish played out on the stout hemp lines rather than snapping the cedar shaft.

Except for the iron spearpoints, this was exactly the rigging described by fur agent David Thompson when he visited Kettle Falls in 1811, and again by naturalist David Douglas in 1826:

"The spear is pointed with bone and laced tight to a pointed piece of wood a foot long," wrote Douglas, "and at pleasure locks on the staff and comes out of the socket when the fish is struck; it is fastened to the staff by a cord." Canadian artist Paul Kane depicted the same style of spear with double-tined points in a painting he executed at the falls in 1847.

According to Manning, the Colville fisherman with whom he bargained was well aware of his spear's value as both an artifact and a tool. "The Indian from whom I got this spear would not sell me the 16 ft. pole at any price but permitted me to cut off the pole just above the spear crotch attachment. These fish spears are not to be found any more in this section of the country."

Manning purchased more fishing tackle of the same general sort, including a double-headed iron point set into a deer horn with the same kind of ball-and-socket insert, as well as

> a single point fish spear made from one deer
> bone, having a socket in one end for spear pole
> and to which is attached a native hemp cord
> about 15 feet long, the lower 30 inches being a
> four strand weave. Cord attached to bone spear-
> head by being wrapped with fine native hemp
> cord and stuck into place by pine pitch. Very old
> and rare.

The Indian hemp cord that makes up the four-strand weave on the lower part of this fishing rig is so even and finely made that it looks as if it came off a spinning machine. This implement, along with others collected by Manning, illustrates the precontact engineering of a culture that had subsisted with the Columbia River salmon at Kettle Falls for upwards of nine thousand years—a fair glimpse of the geologic scale of time that had attracted him to the region in the first place.

A Saddle in the Mud

In the fall of 1905, the *Kettle River Journal* announced that Manning's employers at the Easter Sunday mine were "hibernating" operations because of legal entanglements. Before many weeks had passed, the Easter Sunday's former superintendent had signed on as the deputy surveyor for Stevens County and was at work with a team laying out a new wagon road. His tribal contacts expanded to the Kalispel people (also called the Pend Oreilles), a small nontreaty group living east of the Columbia in the Pend Oreille Valley. The traditional Kalispel range followed the Pend Oreille River north, where it looped across the international boundary to empty into the Columbia, as well as east along the Clark Fork and Flathead Rivers all the way to Flathead Lake.

One of Manning's first purchases in the Pend Oreille country was a beautiful twelve-foot sturgeon-nosed canoe reminiscent of boats admired by David Thompson a century before. "This canoe was made for me in 1905 by totally blind Chief Massalow of the Boundary [Kalispel] tribe, Pend d'Oreille River, Washington," wrote Manning in a brief note. "Ends bound with birch bark and sealed with pine pitch." The craft was made from a single sheet of western white pine bark, turned inside out on a delicately wrought frame of maple and birch, expertly lashed and sewn together with chokecherry bark cordage, and floored with split cedar slats. Manning also procured a four-foot cedar paddle made expressly for the craft by Chief Masselow.

How much William Manning might have learned about the struggle of the Kalispel people to maintain their traditional lands in the Pend Oreille Valley is not known, but for the second time his collecting habit drew him into contact with a key figure during a crucial period of a tribe's transitional history. Masselow had been born near the present Kalispel Reservation, across the Pend Oreille River from Cusick, Washington, in 1826. His father, Victor, represented the tribe in Washington Territory's initial 1853 treaty negotiations, and from that time on consistently argued for a Kalispel reservation on the Pend Oreille River. As Washington's official territorial and then statehood status took hold, Victor discouraged the encroachment of white settlers into his homeland. He also resisted sending Kalispel children to the agency school, because he thought it was important that they should speak the Kalispel language instead of English. Although many of Victor's people had converted to Catholicism when the Jesuit missionaries arrived in the 1840s, the Office of Indian Affairs agent who oversaw several tribes in eastern Washington, Idaho, and Montana, described the Kalispels as "the wildest of all Indians attached to this agency" in 1884.

Three years later, Victor and Masselow, who had assumed the chieftainship from his father, attended a crucial negotiation between the Northwest Indian Commission and the Kalispel tribe in Sandpoint, Idaho. There the presiding commissioner promised that if the Kalispel people would leave their valley home and resettle on their choice of the Spokane, Colville, Coeur d'Alene, or Flathead Reservations, the US government would supply them with land, a sawmill, a grist mill, and farm implements. Victor replied that he would like the commissioners to come and see his home. "The old people that are blind and crawling about. What will become of them? Must I take them and pack them on my back to the Flathead reservation?"

His son Masselow rose and stated, "The little quarter of money you offer will not make us happy. We will not be happy till we die. I am a chief, and these are my people." The Kalispels then retired to council together, and over the next three days "obstinately demanded a reservation within the boundary of the lands claimed by them." The commissioners eventually convinced some of the Kalispel leaders to agree to a treaty ceding their lands, but Masselow refused to sign. Although several Kalispel families did move to the Flathead Reservation in accordance with the terms of the agreement, Congress never ratified the treaty, and many of the Kalispels remained in the Pend Oreille Valley.

After that valley was opened to white settlers in 1890, Masselow continued to resist offers to sell Indian land on the east side of the Pend Oreille River. Reports of ongoing conflicts led to the summoning of a military captain from Fort Spokane to investigate the situation. Chief Masselow met directly with the officer and demanded action, "complaining that his people in the Calispel valley are being abused by white settlers, taking their lands from them and threatening their lives."

Not all of the newcomers acted with such disrespect, and the Kalispels' relationship with the white community was complex. When one settler's cabin burned, Masselow provided the white family with blankets, cooking utensils, and new moccasins for their little girl. Some tribal members seized economic opportunities provided by the changing times. During the early 1900s, a steamboat company advertised cruise trips along the Pend Oreille from Newport to Box Canyon, with one stop at the Kalispel tribe's summer encampment. On these tourist visits, Kalispel women traded briskly in trinkets and beadwork.

During those years, Masselow regularly traveled to see agent John Webster at the Colville Indian Agency to plead for a school and a church to serve his people. Webster reciprocated around 1905 by visiting the elderly chief, whom he described as "old blind Masselow." At about this same time, Masselow was constructing the canoe purchased by William Manning, which must have been a challenging task for an eighty-year-old man whose eyesight was failing badly. Kalispel elder Francis Cullooyah suggests there might not be a contradiction. With Masselow as the overseer, the work could have been carried out by four designated understudies, so well-known that Cullooyah remembers all of their names. These young men had been assigned to absorb the wisdom of their elder for future generations, and it showed up in the well-chosen materials and finely wrought details incorporated into the pine bark canoe.

The next summer, in 1906, Manning attended a Fourth of July celebration at Cusick, across the river from the main Kalispel encampment. At that event he bought "buckskin moccasins & other clothing articles," plus one man's entire outfit. Later purchases included more than a dozen beautiful flat-twined bags, with both precontact and modern designs, constructed of traditional materials such as Indian hemp, wild ryegrass, corn husks, and rawhide. Manning also bought gloves, leggings, tobacco pouches, belts, parfleches, and cedar weaving needles. When Francis Cullooyah thumbs through Manning's list, practically every object reminds him of some scene from his own youth—leggings he saw at a dance; an old woman dipping thumb and forefinger into her tobacco pouch; a belt completely backed with an uncountable number of perfectly stitched blue seed beads.

Everyday items that Manning bought reveal clues about how Kalispel families lived during Masselow's time and long before. The catalog describes a "large spoon made from horn of mountain sheep; used in dealing out portions of food in families." A pair of men's snowshoes with an open weave measured twenty-seven inches long and fifteen wide. A practical lariat had been braided from intertwined strands of black and white horsehair. One well-worn packsaddle was constructed of "deer horns for saddle crotches which are fastened to old pieces of wood by rawhide strings." Horsehide coverings on the wood frame included pockets "in which to stuff grass for the protection of the back of the horse."

"I remember a guy brought in a saddle exactly like that for us to look at when I was a boy," says Cullooyah, who was born during World War II. "It had been buried in the mud for who knows how long before he stepped on it while climbing up the bank from a creek. The whole thing cleaned up pretty good, and we talked about what he should do with it, but in those days everyone was short of money and he ended up selling it." Cullooyah shakes his head. "No telling where it is now."

Other Kalispel pieces from Manning's collection, such as a deer-hoof "spirit rattle used by medicine men," touch the kind of proprietary knowledge that is considered unacceptable for outsiders to possess a century later. Cullooyah passes over these quickly, without comment, as if to emphasize the line between artifacts purchased in good faith and cultural trespass. All that can be said is that nothing on Manning's list indicates he had any sense that it might have been wrong to broach matters of spiritual sensitivity and that his descriptions often attest to the full cooperation of the makers themselves.

Manning purchased several ancient stone instruments from Pend Oreille Valley farmers who had plowed them up in their fields. These he categorized with his geologist's eye, providing a casual tour of the area's complex outcrops and ancient tool quarries.

> Stone ax, granite
> Monzonite stone pestle, perfect shape and condition. Found underground while excavating a basement in side hill on Pend Oreille River
> Porphyry pestel, very old. From Pend Oreille River bank mound on old campground.
> Gabbro pestle
> Quartz monzonite pestel, very hard
> Serpentine round stone for kneading buckskin as it is being tanned

In the years that followed Manning's Kalispel acquisitions, Masselow remained a familiar figure to both locals and visitors. When photographer Edward Curtis visited the Kalispel people around 1912, he took a dramatically posed portrait of Masselow wrapped in a blanket. The blind headman's name appeared regularly in the Newport and Spokane newspapers. One article described how a Jesuit priest traveled to the Pend Oreille Valley on Christmas Eve the year of Curtis's photograph. The priest was rowed across the river from Cusick to meet Masselow and John Bigsmoke, the elderly chief's appointed successor. During a midnight mass performed in honor of the season, Masselow, over eighty-five years old at the time, addressed the congregation in the Kalispel language.

Masselow was officially retired but still active two years later, when President Woodrow Wilson finally signed the order creating a thin slice of reservation land along the Pend Oreille River that included the Kalispels' traditional summer encampment. The canoe builder and leader was well into his nineties when he passed away in 1920. He had helped his people survive the fur trade, missionary, mining, and settlement eras, and he had steadfastly guided them to the return of their homeland sovereignty.

Mattie's Shoes

In September of 1906, William Manning appeared before a judge in Colville to be sworn in as a naturalized US citizen. Two friends accompanied him to witness the proceeding. Age twenty-nine that year, he continued his bachelor lifestyle, maintaining a room at the Colville Hotel while traveling all around the region.

That fall, drawing on his technical mining experience, Manning successfully ran for the joint position of Stevens County surveyor and engineer, and over the next two years he badgered the county commissioners into purchasing a new transit and other equipment so he could carry out his appointed duties. He laid out new bridges and condemned old ones. He recommended road improvements, often along tracks where large mining equipment needed to be moved. He created maps of roads and property ownership, and interacted with the public, attending local booster dinners to explain various projects on the county docket.

Manning also found time to pursue his hobby of collecting, and at some point may have decided to share his artifacts with the public. For one week during the summer of 1908, "the display windows of the Stannus-Keller Hardware Company held an interesting and valuable display of Indian curios," announced the *Colville Examiner*. "Much attention was attracted from passers-by."

After standing for reelection that fall, Manning mitigated a dispute between a railway company and the county commissioners over a road in the Pend Oreille Valley. He helped two college students create an eight-by-twelve-foot relief map of Stevens County for display at the fairgrounds. Then, much to the surprise of some of his Colville pals, he married a Spokane socialite and moved into her home on that city's fashionable South Hill. By 1911 the newlywed sported a new business title to boot: an advertisement offering his services identified him as "U. S. Deputy Mineral Surveyor for Washington and Idaho" and noted that he could be reached through phone numbers in both Colville and Spokane.

Throughout this period, Manning's duties as county surveyor required him to spend time on the Spokane Indian Reservation, where he developed a relationship with William Three Mountains the Younger. For a third time, the ambitious mining engineer came to know one of the seminal figures of a tribe involved in serious questions of territory, removal, and cultural survival.

The Three Mountains name predates the early missionary era among the Spokane people. Spokane elder Pauline Flett explains that the Spokane language renders it as *Chah-tle-hsote* ("three-bare peaks-snag"), which evokes the story of an epic journey. "*Tle* means 'mountain,'" Flett says. "We remember *hsote*, 'a forest of bare trees,' maybe 'a big burn,' maybe 'a storm of some kind.' The original Three Mountains crossed through that bare forest three times going over the mountain. Probably to the coast, we think, because in those days when we said 'the mountain,' we meant the Cascade mountains, and crossing over them meant going to the coast."

As a teenager, around 1839, William Three Mountains the Elder lived with the family of Reverend Elkanah Walker at Tshimikain Mission. The lad left the mission after two years, but as the century wore on, many of his kin were baptized as Protestants. In time, Three Mountains assumed the leadership of a band of Upper Spokanes who spent a good part of the year at the mouth of Latah Creek (also called Hangman Creek), just downstream from Spokane Falls. William Three Mountains the Younger was born there about 1864. He grew into a tall man, "always a head above everyone else" at gatherings.

After a bustling city began to form around the falls in the late 1870s, the elder Three Mountains led his band of Upper Spokanes to a new location on Deep Creek, south of the Spokane River. Blending traditional and modern practices, the people developed a successful agricultural colony there. Three Mountains the Elder continued to play a chief's role in tribal matters of all descriptions until he was killed while trying to mediate a dispute in 1883. His son, still a young man at that time, remained with the Deep Creek colony. He married a tribal woman known as Mattie and continued to farm. Early white settlers in the area remembered the couple well.

One white family who built a log cabin close to a well-used tribal trail that wound through the plains south of the Spokane River grew used to Indians dropping by their place, including a man they called Chief William or Three Mountains William. "He told father and mother to tell Indians they were friends of Chief William's if any Indians ever bothered them," one of the daughters later recalled. She and her siblings often wore moccasins fashioned by William's wife, Mattie.

In 1888, under pressure from the increasing numbers of homesteaders moving into the area, the Deep Creek colony relocated to an area called West End, north of the river on the established Spokane Reservation. Three Mountains the Younger and Mattie developed a farm near the Detillion Bridge, eight miles upstream from the mouth of the Spokane River. "There was a distinctive rock in the river there—we called it Detillion Rock," recalls Pauline Flett, "with the old A-frame Presbyterian church nearby. William Three Mountains's house was just a stone's throw from Detillion Rock." In 1900, the younger Three Mountains was elected as chief of the band his father had led. Like his father, William took active and sometimes controversial stands according to his beliefs. He maintained the respect of both the Indian and white communities, and when he was in his early forties, he accepted a call to serve as a tribal judge.

In 1907 and again around 1912, the Bureau of Indian Affairs' local agent, Captain John Webster, assessed Three Mountains the Younger's work as a judge: "Intelligent, serious, dignified and straight-forward, with courage and integrity," wrote Webster. "By temperament an old time Indian who recognizes . . . the new conditions thrust upon his people . . . he brings to his duties intelligent observation, keen analysis of evidence and strict impartiality."

In carrying out his job as county surveyor, Manning would have met the tall chief soon enough. One of the maps Manning crafted in the course of his duties plotted the lands within the Spokane Indian Reservation, including the location and title-holders for all the original allotments. Census records show that in 1905, Mattie Three Mountains was living with her husband, William, near the proposed road between Detillion Bridge and the Turk Mine, which lay inside reservation boundaries.

Manning surveyed this road three years later, and in 1911, Mattie affixed her thumbprint to an agreement giving consent for a new wagon road twenty feet wide to open along the south boundary of her allotment. In return, an existing wagon road that crossed the northwestern corner of that allotment would be closed.

At some point during these years, Manning purchased a pair of beaded moccasins from Mattie and entered them into his collection records as item number eighty-eight.

> Woman's buckskin moccasins, bought from wife of
> Chief Three Mountain of the Spokanes, who were
> at the time, wearing them. Solid beaded design
> in blue, green, yellow, old rose and purple. 7½"
> long. Beaded on front and outside only.

Mattie had applied the utmost care to those shoes, and the top of each one bears a red rose on a blue panel sewn over with tiny seed beads. Even Manning would have admitted that such showpieces could not qualify as Mattie's everyday footwear.

The collector also purchased at least two other items from the Three Mountains family. The first was an extraordinary flat-twined root storage bag, eighteen by twenty-five inches in size, woven from native Indian hemp cordage and so well used that the traditional geometric pattern worked into the outer wrap had almost completely faded away. The second was a

> bow of ironwood, back lined with deer sinew
> firmly attached by fish glue. Both ends so fash-
> ioned as to form when strung a cupid bow. 36"
> long. Five plain, wooden or target (Bird) arrows

attached. Very old, obtained from Chief Three
Mountain of Spokanes.

Ironwood, the tribe's familiar name for a shrub white settlers called ocean spray, creamwood, or arrowwood (*Holodiscus
discolor*), was well-known for being tough enough to serve as
stock for digging sticks or bows. Once again, Manning's description of an item in his collection perfectly matches a detail in
one of Paul Kane's field watercolors from 1847—in this case,
Kane's portrait of a Spokane hunter he calls Tum-se-no-ho,
or The Man without Blood. Tum-se-no-ho holds a beautifully
fashioned, cupid-curled strung bow in his massive right hand.
The short bow barely touches the ground from his waist, and a
second companion bow pokes out of a quiver draped across his
back. In a separate watercolor, Kane sketched details of a similar
quiver trimmed with bear fur and grouse feathers. Both the bow
in Tum-se-no-ho's hand and the one in the quiver look perfectly suited to the open pine woodlands and basalt scablands
where the Spokanes hunted for such game.

While Manning appreciated traditional designs and craft-
work, he was not shy about mixing in ideas from his own culture. As an active member of the Spokane Shriners club, he
commissioned a Spokane woman to weave the Shriners emblem
of a crescent moon and star hanging from a scimitar onto one
side of a traditional flat bag. Manning did not identify the name
of this craftswoman, but he did describe the bag.

> All in native hemp and wild rye with two native
> hemp strings at top for handles. . . . This bag
> was made for me in 1907 by an old, totally blind
> Indian woman, the widow of a chief of the

Spokanes. She was shriveled and bent into a tiny being and was one of the few old timers left who knew the art of weaving on the outside layer of a double weave fabric without carrying the design to the inside except on the edges.

The world of Shriners and road surveys continued to encroach on William and Mattie Three Mountains, even on their remote corner of the Spokane Reservation. In the summer of 1911, when William strenuously objected to agency attempts to erect a sawmill on the West End, agent John Webster seemed to understand his concern, reporting that "like most of the old full bloods he is adverse to the introduction of certain devices of the white man on the reservation—such as railroads, saw-mills, etc." The following year, when Webster proposed a West End community center based around athletic endeavors, Three Mountains balked again, convinced that the club atmosphere would promote more drinking, which he saw as the bane of res-ervation life. "He is a 'teetotaler,'" wrote Webster, "has a fine ranch he takes excellent care of and during the Fall, after his crops are harvested, he looks for work among white people and can be found busily engaged in the orchards picking fruit, or close to ground digging potatoes."

In 1916, Three Mountains led a council meeting near Detillion Bridge calling for action on the nondelivery of govern-ment funds that had been earmarked for the tribe. Over the next two decades he remained a constant presence in gatherings of Spokane and Plateau leaders as they discussed matters of impor-tance to their people. In photographs of these meetings, he always cuts a fine figure, usually wearing a dark shirt and distinctive neckerchief. His head always rises above the rest of the crowd.

William Three Mountains the Younger died at his home near Detillion Bridge in January of 1937. He was survived by his widow, Mattie, and one son. Mattie lived in the house until the backup of Grand Coulee Dam, completed in 1941, forced her to move higher up on the hillside. Today, although the old bridge is drowned beneath fifty feet of water, the top part of Detillion Rock still rises above Lake Roosevelt, and a campground on the reservation side recalls the Three Mountains name.

Stones and Bones

In 1916, as William Three Mountains argued his tribe's case against the Bureau of Indian Affairs, the Spokane Historical Society mounted a display of local Indian artifacts in a glass-faced cabinet on the third floor of Spokane's City Hall. A newspaper article about the display noted that "W. M. Manning, who has loaned to the historical society the largest single exhibit, said much can be gathered in the way of historical material from the Indians if an effort is made before it is too late. He spent several years in collecting his exhibit." That original display moved several times over the next few years, always under the care of the organization that became the Eastern Washington Historical Society.

In 1925, the historical society's secretary, William S. Lewis, asked Manning to place a value on the collection, in the hopes that his organization might acquire it for their proposed museum. Manning quickly replied with a figure of $1,500 for the entire lot, minus Joseph's pipe, which he had reclaimed the previous year. In the course of assessing his artifacts, however, Manning noted that several items had gone missing over the years, including some stone implements, two woven women's hats, and the very old ironwood bow he had purchased from

William Three Mountains. "This loss of course is that of your institution to whom I intrusted the property," he wrote.

Even so, Manning was willing to make a deal. He told Lewis he would like to keep his artifacts together in Spokane under the title of the "Manning Collection." Secretary Lewis, a lawyer with a deep interest in both the historical society and local culture, immediately informed his board president that they should agree to Manning's offer.

> The loss of valuable articles from this collection
> demonstrates the need for greater care in the han-
> dling and preservation of such collections, and
> for the purpose of cataloguing, and proper con-
> trol thereof I recommend that all historical and
> Indian collections of the Society be placed under
> the direct charge and control of the Secretary.

The deal did not come to fruition, and Manning shifted ground. Following a contentious divorce, he accepted a post as a consulting mining engineer across the Rocky Mountains in Helena, Montana. After he remarried and settled into a downtown Helena apartment, there is no indication that he ever dabbled in the world of American Indian artifacts again.

In the fall of 1930, Manning again contacted the board of the Eastern Washington Historical Society, asking if they would be interested in purchasing his collection for $6,500. Negotiations skittered along until the outbreak of World War II, when Manning became an advisor for the mining division of the War Production Board, assessing claims all across Montana, Idaho, and Washington. It was an important job that kept him on the move until 1944, when he was felled by a stroke while inspecting a corundum mine. Manning's widow took over the dispersal of his artifacts and reluctantly, in 1954, sold the entire collection to the Eastern Washington Historical Society for $750.

With that purchase, the society began updating the catalog made three decades before. Archivists found that while Manning had accumulated scattered items from a variety of tribal traditions, most of the artifacts had been crafted by Plateau people, with Spokane and Kalispel the most numerous, followed by Colville. They also found significant objects made by Coeur d'Alene, Yakama, and Thompson (Nlaka'pamux) tribal members.

Museum curators also discovered, to their dismay, that the collector had picked up, rather than purchased, some of the items, including a handful of grave goods from the Spokane Reservation. The robbing of ancestral graves by white collectors has long been a source of tremendous bitterness among tribal members, but Manning appeared unaware of his trespasses. In his notes he coolly described finding a grave "while tracing some boundary lines . . . about 500 ft. up a steep, coarse slide rock side hill," as well as collecting "Kalispel Indian bones plowed up in the Pend Oreille Valley." Tribal members were acutely aware of such behavior, and they still talk about a human skull that was included in Manning's original City Hall display in 1916.

It's been just over a century since William Morley Manning compiled his collections, and he left behind no writing to indicate exactly what he thought about them. All that can be said, based on his "before it is too late" statement that appeared with his original Spokane display, is that Manning, no matter how much he respected the work and culture of the tribes, felt that American Indians would surely soon be extinct. In the eyes of many tribal members, such collectors thought that by holding an artifact in their hand—whether it was a stone pestle thousands of years old, or a pair of freshly beaded moccasins, or a human arm bone turned up by happenstance—they could somehow "own" pieces of that vanishing history.

But time has proved that Manning and many others were wrong. All the Plateau tribes have survived, and their cultures remain alive. Today the Spokane, Kalispel, Coeur d'Alene, and Confederated Colville tribes play an integral role in the Eastern Washington Historical Society, and they independently own those materials created by their ancestors. Over the last few decades, all human remains collected by Manning, as well as objects of ceremonial or spiritual importance, have been curated and repatriated according to the 1990 Native American Graves Protection and Repatriation Act.

Today, just as the mining engineer desired, the Manning Collection forms a core part of the Plateau collection at the Northwest Museum of Arts and Culture. It is impossible to tell what the collector, certainly a man of his time, would make of the way things turned out. He may or may not have learned to leave the contents alone if he happened to stumble across a grave during the course of his work. He may or may not have been surprised to learn that the three families with whom he had the closest contact, and who supplied him with treasured relics of a culture that he regarded as inevitably on the wane, remain relevant forces in their communities today.

Although the context around many of William Morley Manning's artifacts has changed dramatically, Michael Holloman, a Lakes (Sinixt) member of the Confederated Tribes of the Colville Reservation and past director of the museum's Center for Plateau Cultural Studies, can describe the convoluted last century of both the collection and the people who created the objects in very clear terms. "We will move on," Holloman says, "with the understanding that we are not going to tell the story of these pieces in the same way that Manning did. They belong to the history of the tribes that made them."

So in the end, it is Manning himself who disappeared into the earth, even as his collections have come to constitute part of a continuing and unpredictable story. In ways that he never could have imagined, he served some of his acquaintances well.

VI
RIDING THE HIGH WIRE

Berries

Many summers ago, my friend Tom Bristol and I picked up work haying for a farmer whose place lay on the east side of the Colville Valley. After lunch on one very hot July day, we hauled bales out of a meadow that commanded a view west across the valley to the Huckleberry Mountains. An old and modest uplift, not much more than twenty miles long, the Huckleberries separate the Colville Valley from a north-south stretch of the Columbia River below the old Kettle Falls. The high point of their wavy ridge, named on maps as Stensgar Peak, didn't quite touch six thousand feet. From our vantage in the hayfield, the forested slopes looked empty of habitation, but they were crisscrossed with logging roads and bulldozer scars. Tom came from a mining family and was curious about the scars, while I was more interested in whether those rounded hills might offer good berry picking.

"See that gash straight across?" said the farmer, pointing across the valley to a huge welt of exposed rock. "That's the Red Marble Quarry. You go up there, you'll see how mining worked around this whole country. And if you get to the top of the ridge above it, you'll be into the huckleberries." He made it sound that easy, inviting us to share the mountain's bounty and the span of a whole industry at the drop of a hat.

After stowing our last load of bales in the loft that afternoon, Tom and I followed the main highway north to a turnoff at the mouth of Stensgar Creek. Our county map showed a braided network of dirt roads that followed the watercourse up to Huckleberry Ridge. We chose what looked to be the most heavily traveled left turn and began our ascent. Along the way, we stopped to admire the door to a root cellar set into the base of a little slope above the creek. Some old-timer had laid up fieldstone around the frame, and years of harsh weather had burnished both the door and the rocks in a way that enhanced their air of security. Whoever built the dugout had held a keen sense of both rough timber framing and the subtleties of storing food. Tom and I were recent arrivals to the area, and as we followed the dusty washboarded road up Stensgar Creek toward Stensgar Peak, we speculated on the origin of those place names.

Thomas Stensgar (sometimes spelled Stengar, Steingar, and Stranger) was born in Scotland's Orkney Islands in 1819, during the height of the Columbia River fur trade era. Like many of his brethren, he signed on with the Hudson's Bay Company while still a teenager, hopping aboard its *Prince of Wales* cargo ship when she dropped anchor at Stromness to pick up alcohol and willing apprentices bent for the New World. Stensgar spent almost his entire career around the company's Fort Colvile trading post at Kettle Falls, never rising above the level of assistant trader in a business that by his time was winding down. Stensgar married a Plateau woman about whom little is known except that she died, supposedly of smallpox, leaving her husband with three small children. Six years after the 1846 boundary settlement stranded Fort Colvile south of the international border, Stensgar retired from the only trade he had ever known and settled on a homestead halfway up the Colville Valley along the creek that now bears his name. He was every bit of thirty-three years old.

In 1854, the widower accompanied a friend a day's ride south to visit an old fur trade acquaintance, the well-known trapper, guide, and interpreter Antoine Plante, who had established a ranch on the Spokane River. Plante had been raised west of the Continental Divide by a French-Canadian father and Plateau mother. By the time he was a teenager, he had a job paddling cargo canoes and wrangling horses between fur trade posts on the lower Columbia. In the early 1830s, he was assigned to several of the Hudson's Bay Company's Snake River expeditions, during which he and several of his mixed-blood cohorts drove company bosses to distraction with their "whimsical" ways. After the Snake Country ventures wound down, Plante worked throughout eastern Washington and western Montana. He married Mary Therese Sinsee, of Salish lineage, in 1834, and their daughter Julia was born two years later. The girl was four years old when her parents agreed to an amicable separation, and her father arranged for Julia to live with him on the grounds that she "would have to be provided for in better shape" than her brother, who remained with Mary Therese for a time before also coming to live with his father.

Antoine soon remarried a Flathead woman and began building a horse herd in the Colville Valley. In 1849, the entire family journeyed to California during the height of the gold fever there. Julia was thirteen that year, old enough to help her father pan for gold by pouring water over the earth that he shoveled into a rocker. She also sewed buckskin clothing with her stepmother to sell to the miners for handsome prices. After a successful adventure, the Plantes returned to eastern Washington and located on the Spokane River near a popular crossing point. They raised cattle and horses, cultivated wheat, and planted vegetable gardens and apple trees. Their ranch became a landmark and a refuge for travelers, who feasted on fresh milk and butter from the family's milk cows. Because of his knowledge of the country, Plante was in demand as a guide and interpreter for exploring parties moving through the area. The teenaged Julia, who had learned English, French, and Salish from her parents, sometimes assisted her father.

She was, by her recollection, eighteen years old the summer that a family friend arrived for a visit with Thomas Stensgar in tow. The friend took Julia aside and suggested that the young widower would be a good match for her and that she might marry him. Upon consideration, Julia agreed, and later that year she and Thomas, who was almost twice her age, journeyed to the mission church at Kettle Falls to say their vows. They lived on his sizeable farm overlooking the Colville Valley, where their first daughter, Maggie, was born the next year.

Several other retired fur company employees and their mixed-blood families had also settled in the Colville Valley. Between 1840 and 1880, as the region made a slow transition from British to US control, the birth, death, marriage, and baptismal records of many such blended families were recorded at two Jesuit missions in the Colville country. One of them was consecrated as Saint Francis Regis Mission to the Cree, with "Cree" referring to the mix of European with Plains, Eastern Woodland, and Plateau blood that typified the era. Between 1855 and 1867, Thomas and Julia Stensgar baptized six children at these missions. During the ensuing years they remained engaged in both the emerging white society and traditional tribal culture. They lived on a homestead claim, raised their children in a comfortable farmhouse, and sent them to the district school nearby. Thomas became part of Washington Territory's emerging new order. Stevens County records show that in 1860 he served as an official for the recently formed election board, and from that position, while the Civil War raged back east, he stepped into the role of county commissioner. The couple also maintained a lattice of relationships with many tribal and mixed-blood families in the area. Prominent tribal leaders such as Spokane Garry came to the farm to discuss problems and seek advice. While two of their sons remained in the Colville Valley and farmed land near their parents, another pair married Plateau women and moved to the Colville Reservation. Their daughter Maggie married a mixed-blood son of the Fort Colvile factor and traveled east to the Flathead country; their daughter Nancy married a white man and lived on the Colville Reservation. Many Stensgar descendants are enrolled tribal members on the Colville, Salish-Kootenai, Coeur d'Alene, and Spokane Reservations today.

When Thomas Stensgar passed away in 1891, Julia chose to remain on the family homestead, where she was regarded as "a venerable lady" by the community. During the next twenty-six years, she watched the small town of Addy grow up near her farm and a railroad run through the valley. She watched mining prospectors plant claims all over Stensgar Mountain. She also would have watched the continuous blending of cultures as more and more white settlers came to live among tribal and mixed-blood families. And during the summer, when huckleberries ripened on the hills behind her farm, she might well have been called upon to translate between neighbors who spoke very different languages.

Accounts from several homesteaders who lived in the Colville Valley in the early 1900s testify to the way their families' berry-picking routines mirrored the evolving practices of local Indians. One woman, who grew up on a favorably located and hospitable farm, remembered tribal families stopping by in horse-drawn hacks or buggies each July for a drink of well water on their way to pick berries. Sometimes a lady who didn't speak much English would buy butter from the family's creamery. The young farm girl would listen in on conversations in the Salish language as the pickers parked their wagons along the edge of a meadow and unhitched their horses in preparation for the next phase of the trip. Following much the same procedure as the girl's own family, they would secure a pair of grain sacks to their saddles, then slip square five-gallon tin cans into the sacks so that their berries would not be crushed during the jolting journey to come.

Once they got up into the mountains, white and tribal pickers alike sometimes "threshed" the huckleberries—cutting individual bushes, holding them upside down over a big blanket, and whacking the fruit off with a stick. Everyone thought that such aggressive thinning would help future harvests by encouraging vigorous regrowth. Thick berry patches were essential, because many women aimed to put up one hundred pressure-canned quarts of huckleberries to see their families through the winter. None of them, whether they were returning to a reservation or a homestead, were coming down before they picked those twenty-five gallons and more.

The Dolomite Question

As Tom and I ascended the ridge that commemorates the Stensgars' tenure in the Colville Valley, we did indeed get into berries. The heat had parched some of their leaves toward yellow, so the bushes were easy to distinguish among the other shrubs whose names I had been trying to learn: serviceberry, snowberry, ninebark, ocean spray, buckbrush, and Utah honeysuckle. To enter any promising berry patch, we had to stumble through all of these tangled species, because much of the land on both sides of Huckleberry Ridge consisted of ragged logging jobs growing back in helter-skelter style. Tree limbs and cut tops made it difficult to set our feet when we did find a spot, but we tasted two different kinds of huckleberries, the first, shiny black, and a larger one, stormy blue. Both were so delicious that much time passed before we covered the bottoms of our pails. Each dribble of purple stain, each sharp plink on tin, seemed to settle the riot of the surrounding landscape into a more sensible order. Familiar flowers from my battered field guide, including white scorched penstemon, fireweed, pearly everlasting, scarlet gilia, and sickletop lousewort, fell into sharp focus. Unexpected new ones, such as tiger lilies and a single delicate rein orchid, seemed all the more exotic.

Together we had not filled our first quart before the sun started to sink. With a limited amount of daylight left, the urge to explore overrode our gathering instincts, and we got back into the pickup and rattled up beside the imposing outcrop of Stensgar Peak, then down the far side, following a dirt track that was much the worse for wear. One particularly wicked stretch of road consisted of bare bedded rock that was tilted literally on edge, as if we were driving across the top of a mammoth's laminated molar. Our route improved dramatically as it descended from the ridge to wind through an extensive grove of cedar and grand fir. We were just getting used to the shady dampness when the road broke into a new clear-cut that provided a sudden view straight down on a startling moonscape of exposed stone: the Red Marble Quarry. It took several minutes to absorb how its flat benches had been carved in stair-step fashion up the steep brow of an isolated hill. As the quarry expanded, heavy equipment had run over the hilltop and down the other side, peeling back the earth to create an unruly ziggurat that spilled off in every direction.

Upon reaching the upper terrace of the quarry, we stepped onto neatly bladed gravel. Scores of cottonwood saplings, their dark leaves shining green with balsam, were growing straight out of the crushed rock. Skeins of yellow sweet clover had also managed to push through, and now, toasted by the hot sun, their haunting fragrance drifted over the empty expanse. Where drilled and blasted bedrock walls met the flattened benches, lines of scarlet paintbrush bloomed like marching redcoats.

The angles of these bedded uplifts reached sixty degrees, and more, with some layers of dark reddish-brown argillite standing on their heads at the full ninety: these were the same strata that we had bumped across higher on the ridge. Several of the visible uplifts had been warped by additional pressure, so that their laminations waved like parallel swells in a confused sea. While the exposed stone at the ziggurat's core glowed a luminous dove gray, the edges seemed to have been part of a mad geological experiment. The palette of earthy hues that whirled through these rocks wavered past the basic dove color to eggshell; to ocher and honey; to sage and a greasy gray-green jade; to an oily black tar that poured out in small candied crystals. Overriding all these colors, we saw reds that spiderwebbed in fractal patterns across sheer walls and tabled benches. Their shades ranged from dusty rose to blood red to maroon, all distinct and quite attractive. We tossed a few shapely reddish stones into the back of the pickup, thinking we might find some use for them later.

The Red Marble Quarry illuminates a complex geologic story that began with sediments laid down in a primordial sea. The original layers contained abundant calcium from deceased marine life, and magnesium from chemical processes. Over time, the sediments were altered by heat and pressure, bent by the forces of subduction, and overlain with argillite and quartzite.

The first prospectors to explore the ridge above the Stensgar farm in the 1880s hoped to discover the same glamorous gold, silver, lead, or copper veins that fueled rampant mining fever on both sides of the international boundary and, for that matter, on the other side of the Colville Valley. But this range became known as the Huckleberry Mountains because it provided more dependable food than mineral wealth. Geologists mapped out a definite arc of altered sedimentary rock they called "Stensgar dolomite," part of a scatter of dolomite rocks around the valley. This concept so befuddled me after I arrived in northeast Washington that I finally appealed to an experienced prospector to help me understand its basic meaning. My question, posed in a tavern at a late hour, prompted him to immediately order another round.

"Dolomite," the grizzled miner repeated, sadly shaking his head. "Limestone. Marble. Dolomite. Magnesite. You just can't put them in a box and say this is that, and that is this. There will always be questions."

The man didn't mind reviewing the problem. He explained that dolomite emanates from the basic elements of calcium and magnesium. "Calcite is a mineral with the chemical formula $CaCO_3$, or calcium carbonate, right? You guys must know that. Any rock in a natural setting that contains a high percentage of calcite is called 'limestone.' If enough heat and pressure are applied over time, this limestone can be altered into marble. See?

"Now magnesite," he said, "is a mineral with the chemical formula $MgCO_3$, magnesium carbonate. For reasons I've never understood, they call a rock with a high percentage of magnesium carbonate 'magnesite' too." He went on to explain that geologists have struggled to picture the kinds of conditions that could actually create the mineral magnesite, with the latest theory crediting some kind of hydrothermal replacement at the edge of the hypogene—chemical reactions taking place in superheated water trapped within magma deep inside the earth.

"OK," he continued. "If calcium and magnesium occur in about equal proportions in this kind of rock, they call it 'dolomite.' But academics argue about that too: they call it 'The Dolomite Question.' It's the goddamnedest thing. Dolomite takes all kinds of forms, and now they're thinking it can probably be created in a bunch of different ways. But they still call it just dolomite.

"We could drive all around this county and look at a hundred different dolomite outcrops, and every one of them would show a slightly different color or texture. But that's not what's important, is it? What matters for me is whether you can crush rock out of one place that's consistent, and whether you can find somebody who wants to buy the product. There are paper coatings. Medicals. Fertilizers. Chemical additives. Hell, there's a guy right here in town who's grinding up every color of dolomite he can find to make stucco chips and selling them to the goddamned Canadians. Stucco chips!"

At that point, the miner slumped back in his chair. "This Dolomite Question," he muttered, "it's a hell of a mess."

When a 1902 Washington Geological Survey report tried to categorize the rock formations in the Huckleberry Range, the authors concluded that "The composition of these marbles varies from an almost pure calcium carbonate to an almost pure magnesium carbonate with all grades in between." The predominant color along the entire Stensgar dolomite belt was gray, and the report conceded that it was hard to tell exactly which carbonate was coming out of the various quarries on the mountain slopes. No wonder independent miners of that time touted such a wide range of qualities for the resource.

Cement manufacturers burned what looked like limestone for use as quicklime, a key ingredient in mortar for laying bricks, but their product did not quite measure up to industry standards. Slate makers were attracted to the layers of argillite, a kind of cooked mudstone, that cropped up around the edges of the dolomite. It split well along the colorful laminations but was not as stable as flagstone from Pennsylvania or Vermont. Marble cutters focused on the green and red colors swirled into the basic gray by trace minerals. They cut and dressed slabs for use as headstones and decorative facade work, and sold them to cemeteries and building contractors. Even though the Huckleberry blocks did not hold up as well as the more fully metamorphosed marbles from quarries back East, hopeful entrepreneurs kept pushing their products for more than a decade without any real success. It seemed as though every aspect of the Stensgar dolomite came up a little bit short.

That equation changed with the onset of World War I. The scale of the new conflict called for an immense quantity of high-grade steel, manufactured by the open-hearth process. This method forced preheated air into a furnace, and the elevated heat burned off impurities to create a better product. Open-hearth furnaces were lined with a lacework of refractory bricks that could handle the extreme temperatures without breaking down. And the key ingredient for making such refractory bricks was refined magnesite.

At that time, the US steel industry, based largely around Pittsburgh, imported about three-quarters of its magnesite from Austria, Hungary, and Greece. As soon as the war began, all but Greece's small portion disappeared, and German U-boats soon choked off that supply. When officials in Washington, DC, put out a search for domestic sources, a strange cast of characters who knew about the Stensgar dolomite swung into action. Dove-gray rocks were sent to a Pittsburgh manufacturer of refractory brick, and, to everyone's surprise, their composition matched the company's requirements very well. When the steel men ordered several hopper-car loads for immediate delivery, the rush to control prominent Huckleberry Mountain outcrops was on. Locals soon heard about one hard-up quarry owner who had been offering to trade all his equipment and land to his neighbor in exchange for a beat-up Ford Model T truck. The neighbor kept refusing, then had to watch as company men arrived from out of town and showered thousands of dollars on the lucky quarry owner.

It turned out that the reddish hues of the Red Marble Quarry were caused by infusions of ferric iron. This meant that less iron had to be added during the reduction process, so Red Marble ore was especially desirable to the Pittsburgh mills. The owners of the quarry, who had been trying to sell their reddish "marble" slabs without noticeable profit since the turn of the century, promptly turned down an offer of $75,000 for rights to extract volumes of stone at some point in the future.

While the Great War raged on, the modest Huckleberry Range starred in an ongoing drama involving different companies who vied with each other for contracts, transportation corridors, and production systems. As lower-elevation quarries in the Stensgar formation began to yield riches, the more desirable ore of the Red Marble, hidden away in the high country, lay tantalizingly out of reach for even the most ambitious East Coast operators. But that was before they met an engineer just down the road in Spokane who had a remedy for their problem.

Tramways

Byron Riblet was born in Iowa and grew up as a clever, restless lad. By the age of twenty, he had parlayed a University of Minnesota civil engineering degree into a job designing the Northern Pacific Railway's spur line from Spokane to Pullman. After completing that task in 1887, he worked as a divisional engineer for another railroad line, swimming into fierce competition for routes through the Idaho Panhandle's Silver Valley. When a local economic panic in 1889 led to bankruptcies and labor violence, Riblet slipped west to Spokane, where he focused his talents on the construction of dams, electrical networks, and the city's forty-mile grid of streetcar lines.

Everyone knew, however, that the real money resided with the mining industry. In 1896, Riblet, now thirty years old and with a world of practical experience under his belt, ventured a few hours north into the Selkirk Mountains above Nelson, British Columbia, to investigate a new offer. The Noble Five Mine needed a water-power plant, and Riblet hoped that if he pulled that off, he might interest the owners in a rail spur to haul their ore to an accessible line. It turned out that what the steep terrain really called for was an aerial tramway. Riblet had never built one himself, but he went to school on an overhead tram that had been recently completed for a nearby mine. Within a year, he had directed the installation of wooden towers that crossed a rugged mountainside bearing miles of steel cable woven into a continuous loop, and ore buckets were bumping somewhat jerkily along the wire rope line. It was an instant success.

Over the next few summers, the engineer designed and oversaw the construction of ore tramways all over the Kootenay region of southeastern British Columbia. Local newspapers told stories of drunken oilers getting crushed against the towers and photographed children perched in high-line buckets for the rollercoaster ride of their dreams. Byron Riblet, with no time for such distractions, continued to address several nagging problems that had plagued the overhead concept since its inception. By 1903 he had acquired patents for sheaves, derricks, automatic loaders, bucket latches, and an especially ingenious bucket grip that allowed smooth passage around terminal towers. That same year, Riblet sold his patents and his services to a major wire rope company in Saint Louis and again expanded his reach. He increased the number of his Inland Northwest systems to over thirty and ramrodded the construction of the world's longest tramway until that time: sixteen miles of towers that stretched from a massive Wyoming copper mine to its tall-stacked smelter.

After five years with the Saint Louis firm, the roving Riblet returned to Spokane and established his own business, the Riblet Tramway Company. He married into local society, built a fancy house on the river, and was in a perfect position when the wartime boom in steel manufacturing called for retrieving tons of fresh ore from one small mountain range above the Colville Valley.

In 1917, Riblet Tramway contracted with Northwest Magnesite to build a five-mile overhead tramway connecting its Finch Quarry, located at the foot of the Huckleberry Range, to a reduction plant on a railroad siding just south of the town of Chewelah. Northwest Magnesite's main rival decided to bet on six miles of standard-gauge railroad line that would stretch from its own base quarry to another rail spur. During the race that ensued, construction of the new tracks dragged on for more than a year and cost over half a million dollars. Byron Riblet, who was rumored to be stringing used steel cable left over from construction of the Panama Canal, had the Finch tramway up and running in just over eleven months for $60,000. The tramway's thousand-pound-capacity ore buckets moved twelve hundred tons of crushed rock a day to four large rotary kilns at the Chewelah plant. Inside each giant kiln, a reduction process burned carbon dioxide away from magnesium oxide, reducing the weight of raw ore by half for the hopper-car trek to Pittsburgh. Anyone who witnessed the steady hum of the tramway's cable and the rhythmic flow of the ore buckets as they swooped out of the hills and down to the kilns was mightily impressed.

When the Great Depression hit in the 1930s, Riblet did not handle himself so well. Although he remained president of his company, receipts dried up, and he sold portions of property around his home to stay afloat. When his stately house burned to the ground one Christmas, gossip spread that the tramway titan, perhaps a bit tipsy, had overstuffed his fireplace with gift wrap. He started to rebuild on the same site, but his reputation as a problem drinker began to gain on him. He was arrested for leaning on his horn incessantly in traffic; for refusing to allow a police car to pass him, on the grounds that the officer had no right to speed; and for blocking a freight train at a railroad crossing for exactly the same amount of time that the previous train had blocked him. During the run-up to the Second World War, he made crank calls to Franklin Roosevelt and Adolf Hitler, and showed little interest in his engineering firm. Local whispers had it that the company remained solvent only because a talented young engineer whom Riblet had hired was running the show.

Meanwhile, up in the Colville Valley, Northwest Magnesite managed to ride out the slowdown of the Depression. After World War II erupted, more high-quality steel than ever before was needed, and the orders began to flow again. It wasn't long before the company was thinking once more of the high-grade ore that lay just out of reach in the Red Marble Quarry. In the late 1940s, they rehired Riblet Tramway to extend towers farther into the Huckleberries. By 1949, Riblet's bright young engineer had overseen the completion of the tower line up to the Red Marble Quarry. In his spare time he had developed a lucrative new product by modifying the company's industrial tramways to work as recreational ski lifts.

This innovation allowed Riblet's company to thrive into a new age, but for Northwest Magnesite, the end was near. After World War II, new methods of steel manufacture altered the required properties for refractory brick, and the Pittsburgh mills developed less expensive new sources. When the Northwest

Magnesite operation shut down for good in 1968, the Stensgar dolomite had yielded more than five million tons of ore, and by some estimates the Red Marble Quarry alone still held almost that much more in reserve.

Unspooled

I arrived in the Colville Valley only two years after Northwest Magnesite closed, and many of its key facilities seemed frozen since the moment when the last whistle blew. That was certainly true of the Red Marble when Tom and I stopped there in the stillness of a summer afternoon.

We rambled off the top of the ziggurat and fell in with a well-maintained road that made an extrawide loop before ending at a heavy steel grate set at an angle off the lip of a sidehill precipice. Big wheel chocks remained secure at the edge of the drop-off, where trucks filled with raw ore once backed up to dump their loads through the grate. One worker, usually the newest man on board, would wield a heavy sledgehammer to pound any chunks that didn't fit through the iron bars.

We descended the steep hill thirty feet or more to reach the level where the sized material would have piled up beside a long rectangular building. Wind had torn a few sheets of tin from the roof, but the timbers inside remained impressively solid. This was the takeoff shed for the overhead tramway, and we marveled at Byron Riblet's system of towers and steel cables, still firmly secured in place. The tramway's many ore cars, strung at surprisingly long intervals, waited to be loaded. The cars reminded me of old-fashioned baby prams, solid and squat; the one closest above the takeoff shed had the numeral 37 painted in yellow on each side.

Our eyes traced the elegant double line of cable that sagged between the towers as the tramway system disappeared beyond the up-and-down terrain that led to the Finch Quarry, six full miles away. From there, also standing firm, buckets in place, the next set of towers and cables was poised to make the five-mile run to the reduction plant.

A couple of years later, I would by chance play a very small role in dismantling this operation when I signed on for a temporary stint with the wrecking crew. We released the tension on the cables, allowing them to fly free and terrifying through the trees. We watched a special cable-winding machine, which for all I knew had been used on the Panama Canal, spool the Medusa tangle of wire rope up from the ground. We used an acetylene torch to cut apart the angle-iron towers that had replaced Byron Riblet's original wooden ones, and I picked up the splattered nuts and bolts that had fallen from collapsing struts to the ground, one by one, and tossed them into an old ore bucket. When it was filled to the brim, we would ship the bucket and its load to a Yakima foundry as high-grade scrap steel. It was a rodeo that came and went over the course of a few months, erasing almost all outward signs of the tramway's giant footprints from the landscape. Before many more years had passed, lodgepole pines and Douglas-firs had spread back across the abandoned right-of-way, leaving only the decaying buildings of the tramway's three stopping points—Red Marble, Finch, and the huge processing plant—as witnesses to the reign of that little-known mineral. A few of the former Magnesite workers kept Riblet Tramway ore carts in their backyards as souvenirs, often planted with petunias, but by the turn of the twenty-first century, the original purpose of these had all but faded from memory.

To this day, I continue to drive up and down the Colville River on a regular basis. Every so often, especially in summertime, I make a turn and follow Stensgar Creek uphill, passing through Thomas and Julia's old farmstead.

Julia witnessed the end of the fur trade era and the beginning of the magnesite boom, each of which lasted a mere half century in the Colville Valley. In contrast, some of her special berry-picking places are still loaded with purple in August. I occasionally stop to check in on the root cellar that is nestled so snugly into its hillside, and at one point I noticed that things were starting to get a little rickety around its doorframe. On a recent trip, I was pleased to see that some carpenter had replaced the portal with craftsmanship that would have made the original homesteader proud. The door remained securely closed, leaving me to wonder just how big the space inside might be, and whether a few jars full of huckleberries might still be perched on a cool shelf, waiting for winter.

VII
TERRA-COTTA MAN

Baked Earth

Besano is a small town tucked into the mountains of northern Italy that has been well-known since the 1840s for fossils from nearby Monte San Giorgio. The record there of a warm-water lagoon and surrounding environments from the Triassic period includes ichthyosaurs and other classic sea reptiles beautifully preserved in beds of jet-black bituminous coal. Sequential stable layers allowed early scientists to establish benchmark relationships of rocks and fossils at Besano, and helped set a clock for deep geologic time, which continues to tick today.

Such large-scale wonders have never entirely staved off hard times in the region, however. Luigi and Caterina Prestini grew up in Besano in the late nineteenth century, but they had to cross the border to Zurich, Switzerland, for steady work.

Faithful to the pull of home, Caterina returned to Besano to bear both of their sons: first, Battista, in 1905, then Leno, in 1906. The extra mouths did not help the family's financial squeeze, and the following year Luigi joined the stream of northern Italian men who left their families to seek jobs in America. Like many of his cohorts, he carried artisanal skills along with him and soon found work cutting stone in the granite quarries of Barre, Vermont. Within a year, he sent word for Caterina and the boys to join him.

Even back in those days, it was known in the quarries that few stonecutters worked past the age of forty because the rock dust caused silicosis. Luigi's brother, Federico, had escaped that fate by moving all the way across the continent to eastern Washington, where he established a stump ranch on Half Moon Prairie, just north of Spokane. Federico's letters to his family in Vermont were so enthusiastic that in 1911, Luigi and Caterina decided to join him. Within a couple of years they drifted farther north to Clayton, where Luigi Prestini signed on as a terra-cotta finisher for Washington Brick and Lime.

The lake-bed clay deposits upon which the company was founded reflect a much younger geologic history than the snarling reptiles of Besano. Only fifteen million years ago, the extensive alluvial plain that surrounds Clayton lay on the bottom of Lake Latah. Between volcanic events that saw vast sheets of lava ooze into the area, the edges of this Miocene lake supported a mixed hardwood forest that would not look out of place in the southeastern United States today—everything from ancestral bald cypress, black oak, maple, alder, birch, sycamore, and willow trees to flowering hydrangea shrubs and scuppernong-grape vines. Many of the leaves of this flora that drifted into Lake Latah were preserved in layers of clay that range in color from yellow to blue- and white-tinged gray. This pastel-colored mudstone is composed of small clay particles, which over all that time were never cooked or pressured into harder rock.

A savvy prospector uncovered fossil leaves when he drilled holes with a hand auger to obtain the clay samples in 1893. After testing the properties of the flexible mud, he ignored the ancient forest and began to build a business making brick. His factory and the budding town of Clayton burned to the ground in 1908, but Washington Brick and Lime stubbornly rose from the ashes under the direction of a new owner, A. B. Fosseen.

In a search to understand the subtle variations of his basic resource, Fosseen sank new pits across the breadth of the Latah clay deposits. The startling palette that emerged from one pit had been known by local tribal people and settlers for years but never put to commercial use. Soon dubbed the Paint Pot, its new colors entered the market as specialty pigments of dark orange, ocher, and blood red. But the most valuable excavation carried Fosseen's own first initials, and formed the key ingredient in his mix for the baked earth products known by their ancient Italian name of terra-cotta.

When a state geologist visited the A. B. Pit as part of an industrial survey, he drizzled some of its bluish-gray clay between his fingers. The expert approved of the A. B.'s uniform consistency and fine grain size but found sections to be so plastic and sticky that he wondered if shrinkage might be a problem in the kilns. He attributed a slightly harsh touch to small particles of white mica and noted that their color shone through after the clay was thoroughly dried. This was the kind of raw material that could manufacture success, and indeed, over the next three decades, Fosseen cannily developed a reputation for shipping practical terra-cotta sewer pipe and beautifully crafted decorative panels.

It took skilled craftsmen to create a terra-cotta industry in the wilds of eastern Washington, and many of Washington Brick and Lime's specialists came from northern Italy. That integral relationship was reflected in a 1909 death announcement, published as both the town and the business were bouncing back from their destructive fire. "Battista Giovanni Ponfatto, a native of Italy, 36 years of age, has died of Bright's disease," the notice ran. "Ponfatto was an artificer in terra-cotta, and came from Italy especially to take a position with the Washington Brick and Lime Manufacturing Company at Clayton. He has a wife and four children in Italy." As Luigi Prestini and his family slipped into this world, filling the slack of someone else's sudden departure, steady demand for ceramic sewer pipe and decorative terra-cotta was just beginning to take hold in the Northwest. Both processes required an organic knowledge of the soil, an eye for detail, and the expertise that could only be developed through long hours of practice with the tools of the trade.

The company mined clays of different colors and textures from open pits all around the area, then stored them to dry under roofed sheds. Workers mixed that raw material in exact ratios and pounded it into forms that were air-dried again before moving to one of the four production kilns that had sprouted around the original yard. All these ovens were fired by mountains of pine and tamarack bolts fed into a mammoth boiler.

The first of the kilns was a simple open-air affair used to bake common brick; the second, a beehive dome with forced air circulation that could muster the two thousand degrees of heat necessary to melt a glassy salt glaze onto a style of rough bricks popular at that time. The third kiln took the shape of a long rectangle with an arched roof, like a train tunnel. This tunnel kiln boasted the tallest vent stack on the complex, at 110 feet, and could be loaded from both ends for runs of high-glaze brick or collared sewer pipe. Battista Prestini, the older of Luigi's two sons, used to say that when this kiln reached its maximum heat, flames would lick from the top of the giant chimney.

Separated from these more standard products, the terra-cotta operation occupied a four-story building and kiln that attracted the most skilled artisans at the plant. Here the mix of raw clay, including a generous portion from the A. B. Pit, had to be carefully dried and powdered. Finely ground prefired clay, called "grog," was added to control shrinkage in the finished product. The blend was then hidden in a dark, cool basement to cure.

Meanwhile, on the top floor of the terra-cotta building, special craftsmen called "modelers" studied scaled drawings of architectural details before making their own interpretation of an assigned figure in clay. After adjustments to meet the manufacturing parameters, each piece would be covered with white plaster to create a mold. Fancy trim pieces, bound for commercial projects that included hospitals, banks, and university campuses, were run on a long form like a lumber-molding mill and held together with strap iron. Some large buildings of the period featured a handsome geometric or floral pattern of terra-cotta above every window. Decorative frieze work marked each story, and each cornice called for special elaboration. Certain adventurous architects ordered sculpted artwork, such as gargoyles or animal heads, to enhance a building's distinctive character.

Completed plaster molds would be sent by elevator down to the third floor, where the next crew packed them full of the aged clay mix from the basement—first, by pounding it in tight with their fists, then by swinging wetted cloth sacks full of clay down on the molds, over and over, to be sure that every nook and cranny was crammed tight. After the plaster drew almost all the moisture away from the clay, finishers on the second floor would turn out each mold and chisel the pieces clean. Finally, they cut handholds into the back so the piece could be manipulated through the baking process, the uncertainties of transportation, and during its ticklish installation on a building's facade.

The first floor contained a drying kiln to complete the desiccation process. As individual pieces hardened, they turned almost clear white. That was the signal to load them onto a cart and move forward to the spray room, where glazes would bring out particular colors and sheens. In this condition, the raw terra-cottas were ready to fire, but they were also brittle and very easy to chip. The next crew wheeled them, with extreme care, into the company's special Kiln Number Four.

This huge oven was constructed in the round, with a domed roof and fireboxes around the outside. In the center of the floor sat a separate, smaller domed kiln topped with a circular chimney pipe that ran through the ceiling of the mother kiln—glazed terra-cotta could not, under any circumstances, come into contact with open fire. Because of the odd space created by this doubled configuration, and the equally odd shapes of the pieces to be fired within it, there was always extra room on the kiln floor. Modelers who liked to experiment might add one or two of their own creations to a firing; these might range from a simple flowerpot to more ambitious artistic statements.

Last of all, the operator slid in a flat piece of clay that supported four heat cones. These were calibrated to bend at intervals as the temperature approached two thousand degrees and were placed where they could be viewed when a certain outside brick was removed. It took four or five days of intense heat to make the cones waver, and whoever pulled out the viewing brick had to guard against getting scorched. When the third cone bent down, it was time to extinguish the fire. The crew then allowed the kiln to cool for another four days before gingerly opening the door one small crack at a time. Workers gathered up any damaged pieces to grind into grout and grog, then meticulously measured the whole ones to see if they met the prescribed specifications before they could be finished and packed in straw for shipment. Luigi Prestini, father of Battista and Leno, spent most of his time with the finishing crew during his tenure at the Clayton plant.

Leno's World

For half a dozen years, Luigi hammered at terra-cotta molds with a chisel or an air hammer while Caterina washed clothes for Clayton's lone schoolteacher to supplement the family income. Battista, known around town as Bee, and his younger brother, Leno, helped to raise rabbits and garden vegetables, and bucksawed endless lengths of lodgepole pine for firewood. Bee recalled that his mother was not happy with their house beside the old East Clayton sawmill, but the boys managed to have their fun. They played ball in the sawdust pile, walked to Loon Lake to fish for perch, swam in the flume beside the railroad tracks, and generally pried into whatever mischief they could find. One evening their father brought some clay home from the plant and encouraged the boys to try making a model of their metal piggy bank, which was shaped like a lion. It was Leno who demonstrated an immediate feel for the material, molding his lump into the image of a living predatory cat.

In 1919, Luigi went into the hospital for a stomach operation, then contracted a fatal pneumonia. Times were hard for

Caterina after her husband's demise, and she couldn't seem to shake her grief. She took in a couple of boarders to make ends meet. Bee dropped out of school to work as a water boy at the brick plant for a dollar and fifty cents a day. Leno stuck with the books for another year and a half to graduate from the eighth grade but then never returned to school. Instead of settling into work at the factory, he drifted off to explore the world outside the company town. According to Battista, his brother had always been rail-thin and intense, but he became more aggressive after he returned home. At one point, Leno had a "bad nervous spell" and attempted suicide by sitting in a running car in the family garage.

Bee had worked his way up to the terra-cotta plant by then, pressing tiles as piecework, and he arranged for Leno to come and join him in 1925 as an apprentice in the craft. Within a year, Leno had laid the cornerstone on a new high school in the Palouse and had been assigned the task of mounting a full terra-cotta moose head above the entrance to the Clayton Moose Lodge. That head, which captured the wacky awkwardness of a real bull, stared down at Moose Club revelers until the building was destroyed by fire many decades later.

Battista, for his part, left the company in the late 1920s to work at another brick plant in Tacoma, then moved on to Douglas Aircraft near Los Angeles. The Clayton experience hung in his mind, however, and in his later years he wrote meticulous descriptions of the brick and terra-cotta processes he had learned there. Leno, perhaps to his brother's surprise, stuck with the baked earth, soon rising to the position of chief modeler. Two of his older cohorts at Washington Brick and Lime, Frank Frey and Cecil Sater, served as Leno's mentors, and over the course of the next decade, the three men executed dozens of intricate designs that still draw raves from art deco enthusiasts. Much of the terra-cotta work that appeared as delicate, colorful trim on public buildings is impossible to assign specifically to Frey, Sater, or Prestini, but when the Air National Guard squadron stationed at Spokane's Felts Field built a huge hangar, it was Leno who created a pair of outsized tiles featuring the squad's emblem, an ace of spades pierced by a black dagger. And it was Leno who molded a large terra-cotta American eagle for the parapet of a Spokane armory—a dramatic representation that later was put on prominent display at the city's commercial airport, then eventually returned to Clayton to live again as an advertisement along the highway.

At Washington Brick and Lime, all three modelers dabbled in clay figures on the side, slipping their own glazed pieces into the terra-cotta kiln along with everyday orders of sunbursts and floral patterns. Leno's first efforts tended toward simple knick-knacks, like a bulldog with bulging eyes or a frog on a lily pad, but they displayed a certain style, and he continued to hone his craft. During a lean stretch for the business in the Depression year of 1937, Leno baked a terra-cotta rowboat, glazed in beige and ocean blue. The boat is occupied by two fisherman outfitted in foul-weather gear; while one rows hard, the other turns to blow his signal horn.

When owner A. B. Fosseen saw some of Prestini's work, he commissioned Leno to model Christmas tiles that the Fosseen family distributed as holiday cards through the 1930s. In one of them, a curve in a country road frames a small house, with blue-black leafless trees and a rail fence raised in relief from a background of earth-colored natural clays. Blue-gray smoke rises from the house's chimney to bisect a perfect full moon, and a "Let me live in a house / By the side of the road" ditty in block letters neatly fills the open frame. Another tile features a star of Bethlehem scene with sheep huddled beneath the blue-louvered windows of a stark brown building; behind them, starlight bounces off dry hills. "Merry Christmas" rings out in fancy script, "from the family of A. B. Fosseen."

It was during these years that Prestini emerged as a unique figure in local lore, proving himself time and again to be a gifted design artist crossed with a clever engineer, a broad conversationalist, and a mad adventurer. He seemed to breathe in the essence of northeastern Washington—including the Clayton brick plant and its machine shop; the region's sawmill and mining culture; its mountains, coniferous forests, and glacier-carved lakes; tribal culture and extended trail-horse rides; the taverns, churches, and country music—and spit them back out in ways that were entirely personal.

When Leno decided he wanted to go boating on nearby Loon Lake, he fashioned a craft with cement-sack sails and an iron rudder oriented like the tail of an airplane. The keel was a coffin cover held in place with a length of company strap iron, and Bee recalled how the thin steel would begin to hum as they picked up speed. Any change in their heading would make that strap play a different tune.

After seeing a round diving helmet made by a Spokane machinist, Leno and his friend Burton Stewart used an acetylene torch to shape their own helmet out of a hot water heater, decorated it with a sculpted octopus, and installed double glass to prevent the faceplate from fogging. Adapting a garden hose for an air supply line, they put their odd headdress to work, diving after lost property for the summer lake crowd. Stewart's son recalled that when their original two-cylinder hand pump couldn't force enough air through the garden hose, they switched to a small Briggs & Stratton compressor. Soon the dive team started descending beyond available sunlight, so they cobbled up an underwater flashlight from a six-cell battery enclosed in an aluminum cylinder, with a fuse head to hold the glass and a Model T radiator cap to seal the end. As their dives in Loon Lake approached ninety feet, they ordered balloon cloth from the Goodyear company to sew into a suit that could handle the cold temperatures.

Stewart and Prestini's eccentric operations were just getting warmed up. They salvaged a stainless-steel cream can and fabricated an improved helmet. A beer-barrel pressure pump regulated the air supply flowing though their garden hose. One dockside photograph shows Burton and another pal, in dark shirts, bending over the compressor in the background while Leno, fully tricked out in the white Goodyear diving suit, weighted yoke, and leaden shoes, stares at the camera like Captain Nemo himself. They thought enough of their efforts to exhibit the suit at the Spokane Interstate Fair that fall and to answer a call from the Colville Police Department to help locate the body of a drowned man in a lake north of town. The inventive pair also filed a mineral claim on ground beneath the bed of the lower Pend Oreille River, near the Canadian border. Along a stretch of treacherous rapids known as Z Canyon, the fun-loving friends almost drowned themselves diving for gold.

Leno's hands and mind, working together, seemed to spawn an endless stream of new schemes. He and his brother framed the hull of a speedboat, but in those Depression years, they couldn't afford a motor to power it. He and Burton Stewart climbed mountain peaks all around the region. When the terra-cotta plant shut down for a brief period, they customized a 10-foot ladder and used it to scale the kiln's 110-foot brick smokestack, taking panoramic photographs from the top to prove it. After reading about land-speed records being set at Daytona Beach, Leno fabricated a custom sports car with an airfoil rudder. And at every opportunity, he added his own strange creations to the terra-cotta kiln.

Perhaps owing to his mother, a bit of the reptilian growl from Besano's black lagoon often lurked around the edges of Leno's work. He molded a diver dodging dangerous sharks, and an elf lamp that carried an unsettlingly dark aura. A two-headed mountain climber seemed to teeter toward an abyss, and when Bee asked him about the double heads, Leno replied, "Every time I get to the top of the mountain, my problems are still with me."

Cecil Sater, one of the Clayton modelers who mentored Leno, also dabbled in painting, and Leno began to try his hand with a brush as well. In an interview conducted in the late 1950s, he laid out the progression of his career from modeling for Washington Brick and Lime to painting his personal canvases. "At the plant in Clayton I learned to work with my hands," he explained. "An architect would make a rough sketch of an ornament for a building—an angel in flight, perhaps. But the detail would be up to me. Each man worked that way, and so each developed his specialty in shaping the clay into figures.

"But building codes changed, until cornices and decorations could project only two inches over the sidewalk. The other men started drifting away. I did some drifting myself. And then I started painting."

While drifting, Leno took a job on a sheep train going to Chicago; went on the bum to San Francisco; wandered in Mexico for a while; and worked as a mess boy on board an oil tanker to Hawaii. When he returned to Clayton in 1936, he began slapping house paint on a six-foot piece of plasterboard.

Soon he had produced an expressionistic battle scene depicting a caveman staving off a robot with a head that looked suspiciously like his cream-can diving helmet. Leno called the painting *Civilization—Page 1936*, and it vibrated with an unmistakable sense of conflict. He pressed forward with paint and time, naming new large pieces after succeeding years.

By the time Leno completed the five large panels of *Page 1939*, local curiosity encouraged him to mount an exhibit in the Clayton Cafe. Each panel was a ferociously barbed cartoon satirizing key players with symbolic images of an impending catastrophic war. From Neville Chamberlain popping an umbrella to Benito Mussolini pulling a rabbit out of a hat, the images forecast a dire future for humanity, and many local viewers were put off by the display.

When he finished *Page 1940* the following year, Leno carted all of his *Pages of History* to Spokane, where they were displayed in the show windows of J. W. Graham's stationery store downtown. Within two days, complaints from passersby induced the store manager to move the artwork to the basement. Undaunted, Leno packed up the panels again and drove them to Los Angeles, where Battista had some contacts through his position at Douglas Aircraft. Soon a photograph of Leno standing in front of his *Civilization—Page 1936* graced the arts section of the Sunday *Los Angeles Times*, accompanied by a lengthy article that explained his artistic statement. In the photo, much to the shock of his Clayton cronies, Leno wore a dark suit complete with a perfectly folded pocket handkerchief. He pointed to the robot's bulging helmet with a confident forefinger. "I'm no artist," he told the reporter, "but I can't help thinking."

LA critics begged to differ with the artist's self-assessment, and *Life* magazine photographed his *Pages of History* for an ambitious double spread. But according to Leno, the editors at *Life* were wary of offending European leaders at a time when the United States was still trying to remain neutral in the brewing conflict. The *Pages of History* never ran in the magazine, and Leno was so discouraged that he quit painting for a while. He returned to Clayton, where he confined himself to sketching unruly political caricatures.

When World War II finally spread to America, Leno enlisted. Since he weighed only 105 pounds, he was assigned to limited service at Fort Logan near Denver. During his stay, he completed a book of military cartoons in the style of the time. Eventually, he was shipped to England with a group of P-47 fighters, then transferred to a bomber squadron. Although Leno never talked about it, Battista later surmised that his brother's duties there must have had something to do with designing safety posters and painting battle emblems on the flying fortresses.

After V-E Day, Leno returned home to find Clayton on the skids, and the terra-cotta factory closed for good in 1947. He took up bricklaying and stonemasonry to support himself, and in the 1950s and early '60s he completed a series of fireplaces for cabins around area resort lakes. He never married, but he did have at least two serious girlfriends. He also cultivated an interest in horses, taking long trail rides with local ranchers and cowboys. In order to signal friends he met on the highway, Leno rigged flashing amber light bulbs inside the eye sockets of a horse skull and mounted it on his stock trailer.

Burton Stewart's son recalled Leno as a source of constant entertainment—always smiling and joking, making plans about what stunt to tackle next. When Leno and Burton heard that the venting stacks from the old brick factory were slated for demolition, they stuffed Kiln Number Three's 110-foot chimney with as many old tires as they could find and torched them, just to see black smoke pouring from its top once more.

The two friends also brainstormed about ways to run the Z Canyon rapids, a wild stretch of river just downstream from their 1930s gold claim. At first, Leno conceived of a torpedo-shaped craft that could have come straight out of a Jules Verne novel, composed from various truck and tractor inner tubes stretched across steel piping. He figured that since it was shaped the same end to end and top to bottom, it wouldn't matter how they went through the standing waves. The torpedo was never launched, but in 1958 Leno, Burton, and another friend purchased a bright-yellow Army surplus rubber raft and test-floated it through the Bowl and Pitcher rapids on the Spokane River. Well warned, they outfitted the raft with a splash guard and custom sweeper oars before launching at their mineral claim on the lower Pend Oreille. Their efforts resulted in a rough encounter with rocks and standing waves and ended with a desperate struggle to shore. In a painting of the failed attempt, Prestini inserted a figure of Neptune lurking behind a rock; the sea god is stirring a whirlpool with a log.

Through all this mischief, the artist remained an engaged figure within the community. One spring, when a friend was hired to move the old Clayton Grange Hall to a nearby farm, Leno showed up with his pickup to help drag it across a low-lying pasture. Warm weather had thawed the ground faster than anyone anticipated, and the project bogged down in the slick yellow clays of ancient Lake Latah. Leno participated in two days of this misadventure, then made a colored-pencil sketch titled *Hell at Dawn* that captured the moment when the tattered building finally crested a rise above the bottomlands. While the mover's flatbed truck strains to tow the Grange Hall uphill, an ancient bulldozer bumps its frame from behind. Two pickups, a farm tractor, and a stray dog all pull on extra splayed lines. Every machine, as well as every human and animal, is completely covered with mud.

Vagabond

Prestini did most of his artwork during this period in a converted garage that he called the Vagabond House. Children of all ages would traipse in and out of the studio while Leno painted away, talking a blue streak and often listening to popular tunes that inspired some of his creations. Leno liked to display his latest pieces in a tavern or restaurant, then sit at the counter drinking coffee while he listened to customers' comments.

His smaller paintings varied from quiet landscapes to cultural fables. Though such realistic or romanticized scenes were popular with his neighbors, they were dismissed as "calendar art" by Leno. "I can paint them without half trying," he told a newspaper reporter. "They are for relaxation. Those I like most are my thought-type paintings. They are like myself, the nonconformist."

Prestini's wide circle of friends included other nonconformists who had found their own odd niches in the world. Among these was Homer Holcomb, a legendary rodeo clown; one of Leno's paintings depicts Holcomb wrapping his red blanket around a snorting Brahman bull. The back of the animal's muscular neck snakes down from its bruise-colored shoulder hump toward eyes and nostrils that glow like angry coals. Those same Paint Pot shades recur in the painting *Ghost Riders in the Sky*, conceived when Italian American singer Frankie Laine's version of the song was popular in the late 1950s. As a forlorn wrangler gapes at the night sky, dark clouds sweep a thundering herd up from the bright-orange and blood-red depths of hell.

Leno's more ambitious works used precise symbols to skewer human and corporate greed, the immorality of power politics, and the marginalization of tribal cultures. They wound through dark scenes that explored his constant struggle with female relationships, guilt, and desolation. Several she-devils, surrounded by Freudian trappings and displaying bodies that seem modeled on Alberto Vargas pinup girls, can still make his most loyal supporters squirm. No matter what the subject, all of Leno's paintings displayed his personal sense of color and composition, and his knack for the odd detail. And all of them stirred with the same restless energy that hounded him all his life—as his brother, Bee, said, Leno never could stand to leave anything sitting still.

Around the Vagabond House, Prestini continued to present himself as a stubborn purist, turning down masonry jobs when he didn't feel like working and making a point of telling reporters that he painted for himself, not for money. According to local legend, one evening at the Triple R Diner in Clayton he refused a check for $1,500 in exchange for *Ghost Riders*. Yet there is no question that Leno would have enjoyed more recognition as an artist. In an audiotape of unknown date, his words flow out with fierce intelligence as he sorts through a selection of his paintings, commenting on each one. He contrasts the textured pastel cowboy scenes that were selling in Los Angeles at the time with his own thinner nonlayered technique, explaining how he imparts the lilt of an eye or the crucial moment in a story. He spins a yarn about what happened when cowboy artist Charlie Russell visited entertainer Will Rogers in Southern California. He recalls the flash of orange light in a Rembrandt painting, and the way Michelangelo layered colors to give his

Sistine Chapel figures a sculptural feel. He describes his own work in a way that makes it come alive.

Some people in eastern Washington took notice of his efforts. In early 1961, a show of fifty of Prestini's paintings at Gonzaga University included an appreciation by an English professor. "Leno Prestini may not be a trained artist," he wrote, "nor a genius in color and position, but there is more to art than outward form." The critic went on to compliment Leno's intense compassion for life and his acute awareness of both time and his fellow man, but some outside observers had to wonder whether the only message Prestini absorbed from this backhanded praise was one of condescension.

The Gonzaga show traveled north to Colville, and Leno also exhibited paintings at a Spokane art center and Eastern Washington University. But only a handful sold, and Prestini, now in his midfifties, remained lonely and frustrated. Battista said that "his disappointment in choice of girl companionship and loss of mother plus his false teeth giving him trouble" added to Leno's depression. A doctor prescribed tranquilizers, which Leno did not like at all. But in spite of his problems, he retained his feel for the regional landscape and its people. Those who remember him always remark on his love of coffee and animated conversation. He also continued to practice his craft—when a local auto insurance agent prodded him for a painting in 1962, Leno whipped out a historic scene of Deer Park in exchange for a year's coverage on his Karmann Ghia convertible.

He remained a faithful customer at the Clayton tavern, where no tippler could ignore his full-wall mural that memorialized the town's symbiotic relationship with Washington Brick and Lime. Measuring four by eighteen feet, Leno's version of the story begins with a gangly drillman pulling his twisted hand auger from the earth. The plant founder kneels close to the test hole and touches his fingers to the fine whitish-gray clay stuck to the drill. A tribal figure wrapped in a tight blanket leans against a leafy green tree, looking on sternly, but there is no stopping the process once it has begun. Stumps and ricks of cordwood appear, separated now by raw red gouged clay pits and eroded gullies. Around these grow large glowing buildings and towering vent stacks. A homesteader guides a horse-drawn plow with one hand as he pushes a wheelbarrow of bricks toward a kiln with the other. Flames lick from the top of the chimney above Kiln Number Three, and the stacks behind the terra-cotta building pour black smoke into the sky. A Leno-like vagabond, young and jaunty, heads away from the smokestacks toward the flashing lights of a big city in sight beyond the hills.

A central giant dominates the mural's foreground, split in half between youth and age, flanked on his right by a choirboy, a puppy, and an hourglass full of time's sand. The base of the sand column records the operating dates of the terra-cotta plant, 1907 to 1945, and the curled horns of a ram's head—echoing the Clayton terra-cotta figures that grace the first-floor frieze at Spokane's signature luxury hotel—frame the title of the mural, *From Clay to Clay*. The ram's nose and chin droop across the pages of an open book, on which Prestini has penned one of his introspective poems. "Clay is my heritage," it begins "like this image of the craftsman in clay."

In his arms, the chiseled craftsman in the center of the mural cradles a finely ornamented art deco office building, but a long rough chain around his shoulders binds him to the picture frame itself. To his left, the sands of a second hourglass have almost run out, and his companions have been reduced to a nodding drunk and an exhausted old dog. Behind them, the aged vagabond returns from the city to a snowy, ruined landscape and a shuttered brick factory. A drunk man at the bar represents both Leno's cherished mentor Frank Frey and the pathos of the company town; the vagabond's struggles and the entire chaotic world. "I too, am chained to this picture," reads the second page of the poem, "until the time when clay shall inherit me."

Originally mounted in Matt's Tavern in Clayton, *From Clay to Clay* is only one of several Prestini originals that graced the walls of businesses in the small town. In the mid-1950s, when a fast-moving fire tore through Clayton's single main street, flames destroyed one of his murals that hung over the produce section of the local mercantile. Racing ahead of the inferno, anxious citizens descended on Matt's Tavern and rescued Leno's painting of the brick plant. All of its disparate elements—from the leering company founder to the grim reaper leading a besotted Frank Frey to his grave; from a quiet Catholic church to the blue star in the window of an honorable war veteran; from the snow-covered terra-cotta building to the eerie purple and ocher bands of night's descending sky—were rolled up on an ax handle and carried out of harm's way.

In the early months of 1963, Leno drove to Los Angeles to visit Battista. There, Bee said that his brother acted "very nervous and unhappy, then painted a couple of paintings with a spatula and didn't like them so he threw them in the trash." As Leno prepared to return to Clayton, Battista rescued the pieces from his garbage can and made his brother promise that he would go see a doctor as soon as he returned home. Two days later, Burton Stewart called to say that Leno had shot himself and was in the local hospital with a bullet wound to the head. He lingered for almost a month but never regained consciousness.

Battista refused to let his brother's memory fade completely away. Over several summers, with the help of friends in the Clayton community, he and his wife constructed an A-frame building for a museum. They combined a large selection of Leno's work with their own lifelong accumulations from Washington Brick and Lime and gave guided tours all through the 1970s and early '80s. When Bee grew too old to keep up the museum, a younger generation of descendants auctioned off its contents, but buyers within the family managed to retain most of Leno's paintings and many of his effects.

Neal Fosseen, the son of A. B., served as the president of Washington Brick and Lime after World War II as it fought its way through bankruptcy, building trends, and consolidation with other Spokane brickyards. In an interview, Neal Fosseen clearly evoked the atmosphere around his family's Clayton operation in the 1930s, when fine terra-cotta was being modeled up on the fourth floor. He snorted audibly when Leno's name was mentioned—"sometimes Prestini could be a little tough to deal with," he remarked. But he remembered the fun parts as well. Fosseen recalled that Leno would slip his own handmade terra-cottas—pieces such as *Two Fishermen in a Boat*—into the kiln just before it was sealed off for firing. And he counted off the years during the 1930s when his family delivered Leno's picture tiles to friends as Christmas cards.

When asked what he thought of Leno's more ambitious paintings and the way his reputation as an artist had swelled beyond Clayton, Neal Fosseen snorted again, quietly. "That's not the way I think of him at all," he said. "To me, he was just Leno."

Fosseen then recounted how the realities of the Depression in the latter 1930s meant that there were often no orders for the terra-cotta plant to fill. During those periods, Leno would be laid off to pursue whatever caught his fancy, and, Lord knows, he did all kinds of things. But if a call came in, Prestini would dependably show up at work and resume his post as head modeler. "Look," said Neal Fosseen. "He was a terra-cotta man."

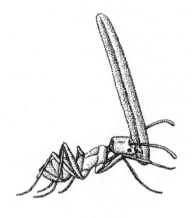

VIII
Sisters

Kicking the Mound

The spring morning had been cool, and at first the gentle mound that rose beside the big ponderosa pine seemed lifeless. But as glints of sunlight began to filter through the trees, a few ants emerged from the pile.

"Red ants!" hollered one of the students who had been watching the mound.

"Actually," I said. "They're called 'thatching ants.'"

"No, no. Red ants. Let's watch 'em and see what they do."

The students policed themselves for the next several minutes, barking at anyone who attempted to pick up a stick or edge closer for a kick. We talked about a golden currant bush that the colony had engulfed, and the way each of its profusion of yellow flowers might grow into a fruit over time. Were the ants going to change that? Would they eat the sweet currants?

One girl spread her arms wide, palms facing each other, then swung them ninety degrees to gauge the breadth and height of the mound. She judged the pile to be almost four feet in diameter and more than two feet tall at its peak. Another member of the group was sure that there was a queen hidden deep within, whose responsibility involved laying eggs.

As more ants trickled into view and began to spread across the surface of the half globe, one boy plucked a loose individual from the edge and held it up to his face for examination: "See?" he sneered at his partner. "They're not *all* red—only the head and middle. The back's shiny black." He paused, twitched his nose, and held the flailing ant close to his face. "What's that smell?"

Now all the kids were leaning in. The ants were still moving slowly enough that the students could marvel at their different sizes, but it wasn't long before one student got nipped. With that, the circle of humans jumped two steps back.

"Fire ants! They'll sting you!"

"Thatching ants," I said. "And it's a bite, not a sting."

The victim, sort of in agreement, shook off his wound and blended back into the class. Two students who had ignored the casualty pointed to a black hole that was opening on one side of the mound. We could see the way workers were moving material this way and that, enlarging the hole.

"That one, see, he's got a little rock!"

I slipped in the fact that since every ant moving within our view was a female, it must be a *she* carrying the little rock. One of the girls who had first noticed the tunnel entrance pondered the seething mass of sisters. Then she straightened up and backed away from her classmates. The girl extended her left arm straight out in front of her face before deliberately raising her right arm past her ear at a forty-five-degree upward angle. She bent down to grab a handy stick and repeated the pose:

"Kendo fighting position! Hah!"

She broke rank to march around the outside of the circle: stick aloft and stiff-armed, she deftly imitated an ant she had watched parade with a fragment of a pine needle. *Man*, I thought. *If only Dr. Hansen were here to see this.*

But I couldn't dwell on the professor's absence. Another student had tweezered a single ant between his fingers and stuck it in a girl's face. She drew in a sharp breath, then sniffed again. "It's lemon," she said. "That's the smell!"

Someone else had a brother who had been through Air Force survival school, where he had been taught that in a pinch, he should drink ants crushed in water to keep going. The recruit swore they tasted like lemonade, and it sure beat drinking your own urine.

"Pissants!" came the quick response to that news.

"Thatching ants," I said. "But they do smell like lemons."

"Pissants!"

Energized either by the human commotion or the heightening sun, the level of ant activity around the mound steadily increased. More scouts combined to push back the perimeter of kids. Ant kendo masters moved materials identified by student eyes as bits of bark, broken pine needles, twigs, pebbles, and grass blades. Several lugged tiny bobbing jewels that turned out to be drops of hard pine resin reflecting the sun. Others hauled cricket legs and—much to everyone's delight—an occasional dead ant. Around the upper reaches of the mound, two more tunnels opened like chanting Buddha mouths.

"It's alive," one boy muttered. "The whole thing is alive!"

Several were still shouting "Pissants!" when a teacher arrived to edge the group away from the mound toward the next station on their schedule.

Inside the Colony

Dr. Laurel Hansen is a member of the biology department at a community college in Spokane. She has also coauthored a monograph on North American carpenter ants, genus *Camponotus*, that delves into their life history on every conceivable level. I initially heard about her when neighbors called an exterminator to deal with an ant invasion in their kitchen. Dr. Hansen showed up to assess the situation—as a longtime consultant with many of the area's pest control companies, she often joined operators in the field. Her brief appearance set the neighborhood abuzz, because, several friends later informed me, this ant lady had a reputation for solving difficult cases.

With the goal of learning a little about the thatched mounds I kept seeing in the woods, I gave Dr. Hansen a call. She invited me to visit her laboratory between classes and did not waste any time with chitchat when I arrived.

"*Formicas*," she said in a friendly way as she shook my hand. "That's what we call the thatching ants. And, no, I don't really know anything about them."

This was not the answer I had expected to hear. "Aren't you the expert?" I asked.

"Some people think so, but it's really all I can do to keep up with carpenter ants," Hansen said, then added, "Lucky for us, I have a student who is behind in his work and looking for extra credit." She stepped toward a standard-issue metal garbage can and motioned for me to pull up a chair alongside hers.

Just the previous week, she had noticed a thatching ant mound at the edge of campus that lay within the staked boundary of a proposed parking lot. Before the bulldozers arrived, Hansen had dispatched her student, Eduardo, armed with a shovel and a heavy plastic leaf bag, to the spot. Following instructions, he had dug as deep as he could—at least as far down as the mound was tall—and returned with a bag full of dirt and thatch, along with an untold number of angry red-and-black ants. That had happened a couple of mornings ago, and Eduardo was due back to inspect his labor any time now.

Dr. Hansen and I peered into the can. We sat quietly for a few minutes, watching an unsorted maze of ants scurry across the throbbing mass of duff. Several outliers had tackled the side of the can and were making their way to the top. Hansen grabbed a jar from a nearby countertop and redaubed the inside of the can's upper rim with a slippery mixture of petroleum jelly and mineral oil so that none of the emerging prisoners could ascend the lip. "It's true," she said as she neatly pinched a single female worker between thumb and forefinger and inspected it with a hand lens she carried on a string around her neck. "I don't even know what these things are."

Formica is the largest genus of ants in North America, with well over one hundred named species. These are often lumped into seven rough groups, with *rufa* covering most of the red-and-black ones in the Inland Northwest. But major taxonomic revisions were under way. A British Columbia colleague of Hansen's thought he had identified seventeen different kinds of thatching ants spread across the province. That sounded like a few too many to Hansen, and she had decided to call them all *Formicas* for now. I was agreeing that that was fine by me when Eduardo arrived and pulled another chair to the lip of the garbage can.

"Well," said the professor to him. "Looks like you did all right here—a fair sampling of the colony, and it's beginning to come back to life. But it'll be a while before we find out whether you managed to capture a queen."

The three of us sat around the barrel and watched the ant sisters scurry about, making order out of chaos. Hansen waited for a while before asking, "Does any of this make sense yet?"

Neither Eduardo nor I had an answer for that, and neither of us budged until Hansen leaned forward to focus on something that looked like a tamarack needle, bobbing above the crowd. A female worker carried it with one foreleg stretched straight out in front of her and the other raised at a forty-five-degree angle, so that as the ant marched resolutely across the pile, the needle flowed forward like a war banner. Eduardo followed the ant's actions carefully before finally nodding his head.

Nuptials

During several succeeding visits, my lessons took place against a similar backdrop of complex social activity. An intern would be tidying up with one eye on a tank of newly hatched walking sticks. One student would be laying out papers across a lab table; another would wander in to try to cut some kind of late-work deal similar to Eduardo's garbage can project. Various faculty members dropped by with news, and once a custodian knocked politely to explain how he had handled the recent escape of a Madagascar hissing cockroach. My contribution was to collect any references to ants that I ran across in early fur trade journals or tribal stories and present them for Dr. Hansen's consideration.

In April 1806, for example, as the Corps of Discovery paused at the edge of the Columbia River Gorge, Lieutenant William Clark welcomed spring activities there. "The air temperate,"

he wrote. "Birds singing, the pizmire, flies, beetles, in motion."
Could the word "pizmire," I wondered, offer a clue to our slang
term "pissant"?

"Maybe," said Hansen, politely making it clear that she had
seen the quote before. She said that to most people, a "pismire"
means any large ant belonging to the group that, like both carpenter and thatching ants, sprays threatening invaders with
formic acid. She thought it was a Scandinavian term, but she
heard it all the time in reference to the big black carpenter ant,
Camponotus modoc. She was not entirely convinced "pissant"
grew out of "pismire," but she guessed it did make a little sense.
"They live in a chemical world, after all. We're so dull we think
most things smell the same."

Other mammals can receive such chemical messages more
clearly. Across the Columbia Basin, tribal people utilized con-
venient depressions in open talus slopes as storage pits for roots,
berries, and meat. I had heard that they would sometimes line
such pits with duff from an abandoned thatching ant mound,
because the scent of formic acid repelled any chipmunks or coy-
otes that might have designs on the food. Dr. Hansen was not
surprised. "Not many animals want to mess around with ants,"
she said.

Sometimes people did, even if it was by mistake. In early
summer of 1858, John Keast Lord, a naturalist for the British
team of the Northwest Boundary Survey, was plying his trade at
Kettle Falls on the Columbia River. Over the course of a long
evening he watched swallows, swifts, and common nighthawks
swoop and boom above the river. As was his habit, Lord shot
down one of the nighthawks and upon dissecting it discovered
that "its stomach was gorged with winged ants—a flight of these
insects had, I imagined, attracted all these birds."

J. K. Lord's tale struck a chord with Laurel Hansen, because it sounded to her as if the nighthawks might have been feeding on a nuptial swarm of carpenter ants—a key moment in the annual cycle she had traced for her doctorate. During one frantic period of her studies, Hansen had duct-taped many yards of mesh into a cocoon that enclosed her entire lab. When winged male and female breeders, called "alates," emerged from a carpenter ant colony she had kept all winter, she watched them crawl up onto the highest desks and chairs in the lab and make the characteristic twisting twitches of their abdomens that meant they were ready to swarm. As the alates began to fly, she chased them around, trying to record the first detailed scientific observations of *Camponotus modoc* mating behavior.

"One thing about Mr. Lord," she observed. "His June date seems a little late compared to the carpenter ant flights I've seen in my time. Could something have happened that changed their timing since the 1850s? I mean, that isn't even yesterday for them."

The alates in that nighthawk stomach launched Hansen into the concept of "Ant Time." According to very clear amber fossils, ants diverged from a common wasp family relative almost a hundred million years ago, during the middle Cretaceous period. By the early Eocene epoch, fifty million years later, their social kin already dominated the insect world. Today there are species of bulldog ants in Australia that don't appear all that different from fossilized Eocene individuals. Such deep-time connections make it difficult to grasp the time scale that ants inhabit, which is much more geologic than human, or to separate the threads of any particular type's life history. For instance, Hansen had identified both pavement ants and pharaoh ants wandering around her campus. Both are cosmopolitan species, but up to now no expert has managed to pinpoint either kind's exact place of origin.

"Think about it," suggested Hansen. "How did they get here?"

It was easy to visualize some invasive species riding up from South America in the last century, hidden on a banana boat. Another queen might have ridden a storm system east from the Philippines a thousand years ago, or crossed from Asia to North America via Beringia in people's belongings ten thousand years before that. But bulldog ant queens might have ridden separate tectonic plates while our present major continents slowly rotated away from Gondwanaland, tens of millions of years back.

A Practical Lab

During my ensuing visits, Dr. Hansen showed me an array of carpenter ants that she kept among the assorted live study insects that occupied a narrow alcove beside her laboratory. The ants never wandered far from a supply of decomposing wood that provided their shelter and food, and she could use them to illustrate various points to her students. Early on, she handed her magnifying loupe to me so that I could get a sense of how efficient a carpenter ant's stout plier-like mandibles are for excavating old firewood from the inside. Then we moved back to the garbage can to contrast those pliers with the needle-thin pincers of Eduardo's thatching ants, designed for carrying things or spearing larval prey. "You can tell the different shape by the feel of each one's bite," she assured me. In another of her cabinets, we looked at drawer after drawer of wood samples that carpenter ants had chewed and polished neatly along each tree's growth rings. Most of the samples came from infested houses that Hansen had visited, but on a deeper level, the sister ants had excavated those galleries and chambers as they carried out their appointed work of composting Earth's decaying biomass.

Carpenter ants and their relatives are so common in Northwest forests that large predators such as pileated woodpeckers rely on them for a sizeable portion of their diet. Thus it stands to reason that as long as people insist on putting up framed lumber homes in wooded habitats, the ants are going to pose an economic problem. Research has proved that in northern latitudes, carpenter ants inflict more structural damage than termites—a statistic that touches the reason why Dr. Hansen was originally drawn into studying these ants.

"Growing up on a farm, I was always interested in the social insects," she explained. "When I told my advisor I wanted to investigate termites, he said, 'Everybody looks at the structurally invasive termite mounds in the southeast. But nobody knows anything about the ants that are all around us right here. Especially carpenter ants.'"

That set her on track, and carpenter ants proved to be a good subject, because the *Camponotus* genus contains a reasonable number of well-defined species. In most of them, the many thousands of female workers, plus a few males for breeding, are born into single-queen colonies and remain extremely nest-faithful—any outsider that wanders in is immediately killed. Carpenter ants are polymorphic, meaning that the sisters grow into a range of sizes; this allows them to successfully tackle jobs of varying scale. They are a dominant species, with enough large workers to overwhelm most other kinds of ants when their territories conflict. And they are wonderfully adaptable even as they pursue their single-minded ways: female scouts exploring random paths through forest duff can switch immediately to the straight line of a foundation sill board or aerial telephone line if it leads to accessible wood on the other end. During the course of her studies, Hansen learned to take real satisfaction from the ants. She observed one *Camponotus modoc* colony that thrived for twenty-one years tucked deep into the base of tree on a bank over a pond until a storm toppled the entire nest into the water. A single queen, after one night of fertilization inside a nuptial swarm, had supplied that nest with regular new eggs for more than two decades.

Once Hansen understood carpenter ant life history, people began to ask her for advice about how to get rid of them. When she realized that she had a knack for putting that knowledge to use, she decided that a practical job—like visiting some horrified family's alate-strewn bedroom and offering steps to remedy the situation—suited her better than abstract research. "We call it 'applied science,'" she said.

Although Dr. Hansen had harsh words for pesticide companies that favored poisons over accurate data, she sometimes ran lab trials for businesses that had a more enlightened view of their work. She was always in demand—there weren't that many people around who knew how to wrangle ants—and as someone who tried to solve most problems by convincing the ants to go somewhere else, she was particularly interested in fresh concepts.

On occasion, however, she could also be talked into more traditional experiments. Once I entered the lab to find every inch of table space covered with clear plastic sandwich boxes. An assistant had carved perfect circles from the lids of the containers before smearing their tops with a Teflon component to halt potential escapees. Hansen had loaded each one with the proper amount and strain of poisonous test bait, then somehow coaxed an approximately correct number of tiny sugar ants inside.

While the professor made her daily rounds with a clipboard, counting dead ants and making sure all else was in order, we caught up on various threads of news. Hansen had recently traveled to Southeast Asia for a conference, where she had mingled with peers from all over the world while visiting some astonishing ants in both city and forest. Back home, she had run a couple of workshops for professional pest control workers—"nozzle jockeys," as she liked to call them, because until they met her, most thought their job began and ended with a backpack spray tank. "I can call them that," she said, "because I listen to them and we can joke around. We're trying to accomplish the same thing after all, and it's a lot easier if you know what you're doing.

"All this business"—she waved at the plastic boxes—"we have to think about it because ants are so intertwined with people. How many ants can you tolerate, that's what it comes down to. Everyone seems to have a different threshold."

I confessed that I had never lived in a house where a few winged carpenter ants didn't appear inside the kitchen each spring. Unless their numbers grew into the hundreds, we managed to coexist. Hansen nodded. "Yet for some people, and for some businesses," she said, "one single ant turns out to be too many."

The Box

Dr. Hansen's particular knowledge has gained her many friends, and one of them built her a glass ant farm about three feet square and the thickness of a small bookshelf. It came complete with a screened lid and a cleverly rigged water system that dripped through bottle caps mounted beneath the cover. Early one fall, Hansen had a couple of her students load the box with an orphaned mound of thatching ants, then heft it onto an open countertop in her lab. Because she wanted to put the colony to sleep for the winter, Hansen asked them to push the box flush against the wall and to cover the exposed side with heavy black construction paper. When I swung by one November afternoon, she stripped the paper off so we could have a look.

The ants had not spent all their time sleeping. From our side of the glass, we could see that they had layered the duff into a marvelous tunnel system, irregular but highly organized, like a crazily warped geologic syncline. In places where the tunnels occasionally swelled into larger chambers, Hansen tapped her forefinger against the glass. "Haven't found any eggs or pupa yet," she said. "Don't know if there's a queen or two hiding in there somewhere. But we'll see once they really get going in the spring."

Thatching ants are very different from carpenter ants, in that the female workers tolerate multiple queens in the same colony—what Hansen called "polygyny." That means that new colonies can bud off an original nest into a scatter of smaller mounds. If a worker from the farthest related mound wanders back to the original colony, the sisters there allow her to enter unmolested. Such behavior runs utterly counter to that of single-queen *Camponotus* species, whose workers immediately attack any outside intruder, for territorial protection. Since polygynous ants have the potential for rapid expansion, troublesome invasive species always belong in this category. South American fire ants, whose red mounds dot fields across the southeastern United States, and Argentine ants, which apparently arrived in New Orleans in coffee sacks a century ago, have both spread across entire states like a slow-moving ground fire, and rank high in any local manual of insect problems. Native thatching ants, whose distribution circles the entire Northern Hemisphere, tend to remain more in balance with the habitats around them. They rarely get more than a passing nod from the pest control business.

"Balance," said Hansen, "might not be exactly the right word."

She told me about an extended colony of *Formica rufa* thatching ants in the Blue Mountains of northeastern Oregon. Researchers termed it a "supercolony" and had found reports of similar occurrences from Europe and Japan. The cluster of mounds, bounded by an abandoned sawmill and a commercial hot springs, covered ten acres of mixed coniferous forest. Several timber tracts around it had been logged to harvest trees damaged during a recent destructive outbreak of the western spruce budworm.

To test whether all of the individual anthills in the area had split off from one original queen, the researchers took workers from random mounds and reintroduced them across the colony. All were readily accepted by their sisters. But worker ants collected from mounds outside the area were immediately pinioned to the ground, then bitten and sprayed with concentrated formic acid.

The biologists mapped the breadth of the supercolony, counting more than two hundred fifty mounds randomly scattered throughout the acreage. Just over two hundred of those mounds were currently active, and the separate colonies varied widely in size. A formula was devised to calculate the volume of individual mounds above- and belowground, with the seven largest hills estimated to harbor more than one million ants each. As the total population approached sixty million individuals, the researchers realized that the food required by that number of ants would total close to a thousand pounds a year.

Thatching ants consume a host of different foods, depending on need and availability. Some colonies maintain large aphid herds, both to harvest the honeydew processed by these tiny suckers of plant juice and to eat individual aphids directly. But the épée-shaped mandibles of *Formica rufa* ants are perhaps best suited for skewering caterpillars and other insect larvae— say, for example, developing spruce budworms.

Any thatching ant mound is a key predatory factor on the insects within its sphere, and this supercolony provided researchers with an opportunity to gauge that influence on a very large scale. When biologists ran the numbers, they realized that the combined population of all the mounds could easily consume the number of spruce budworms required to defoliate a forest stand of comparable area. Subsequent surveys indicated that the acreage within the ant supercolony had sustained significantly less damage from the spruce budworm outbreak than surrounding forest tracts.

In an attempt to measure the density of the thatching ant population outside the study area, researchers walked transects through surrounding patches of defoliated and logged-over Blue Mountain forest. In all, their census covered one hundred miles of trails. Along that entire length, they did not find a single ant mound.

"That's what I mean," said Dr. Hansen, "when I say I don't know anything about thatching ants."

She reached up to lightly thump the top-side watering system, causing the bottle caps to sprinkle drops on top of the thatch. "They're supposed to be in torpor, but a few always come up to meet the moisture."

Sure enough, individual workers immediately began to emerge from the desiccated tunnel system to check out the fresh water drops. As they skittered back and forth, one stumbled across a pile of dead ant bodies that lay heaped in a corner. "Oh, yes," said Hansen. "Part of getting organized is separating out all the recent mortality. If you watch long enough, you'll see some workers hauling up the day's bodies."

As she spoke those words, I thought of a story told by a man named Barnaby, a member of the Saint Mary's band in the Kootenay region of southeastern British Columbia. More than a century ago, Barnaby recorded a long and complicated Raven tale for an anthropologist. As the story unspooled, Raven lost a son and a daughter in separate grisly accidents. Raven was recounting their fates to a village chief when Ant suddenly appeared to act as the designated gravedigger. "Ant tightened his belt in order to bury the dead," said Barnaby. "He almost cut himself in two, and was small in the waist after that." Laurel Hansen and I looked at the ants in her glass case, both alive and dead, and I wondered what else Barnaby understood about them.

Almost Alive

In 1810 French zoologist Pierre Huber observed that individual thatching ant mounds were cleverly engineered to present a favorable exposure to the sun. He realized that the amalgamation of materials on the outside of each mound provided protection against hard rain, wind, and extremes of temperature and humidity. Inside the structure, rich organic materials supplied insulation and food for the colony's interconnected shafts, galleries, and egg chambers that reached just as far beneath the ground as the top of the mound rose above it. It was Huber who first suggested that the primary function of these mounds might be microclimatic regulation. His notion helped me lure Dr. Hansen into an August stroll through the same stretch of piney woods where, earlier that spring, my group of students had gathered around a busy mound of thatching ants to watch them operate in the wild.

In the late summer's sun, several of the older ponderosas showed the thick outer bark that glows like a ruddy sunburn and supposedly marks the passing of a tree's first century. Bunchgrass filled the space between them, with a few late lupines and heavily scented yarrow plants standing out among the tussocks. The serviceberries had shrunk to tiny black raisins by this point in the season, but hawthorn berries were just beginning to come on.

Dr. Hansen stopped at a good-sized pine snag to pry on the fissures between its bark. Plates popped off like pieces of a jigsaw puzzle, filling the air with a vanilla scent. Before many moments had passed, she paused and drew her head back from the tree. Looking for big black carpenter ants, I leaned in but saw nothing. Then a smell like rotten coconut began to overtake the delicate vanilla of the pine. Following Hansen's gaze, I spotted smaller ants, lots of them, traversing the freshly exposed layers of bark.

"Velvety tree ants," she said. "Look how they're running with their butts up in the air. They're spraying a pheromone that makes that rotten smell."

The ants were so small and quick that it took several more moments to see that each one had its abdomen tilted up at an awkward angle. Dr. Hansen snatched a single worker out of the mob and trained her lens on the soft abdominal hairs that inspired its name.

On the next tree we came to, the simple turn of a downed limb exposed a carnival dance of another small species of ants, and Dr. Hansen wandered over to appraise them. "We call these crazy ants. See how long their legs and antennae are in proportion to their bodies? That's what makes it look like they're running crazy. They're a tramp species, always hitching rides from one place to another. Customs agents see them all the time. No idea where they originally started from. No idea where they're going."

"But if these crazy ants rely on humans to move from one place to another," I asked, "what are they doing out here in the woods?"

"Well," replied Dr. Hansen, "maybe they know more than one way to live."

It was late afternoon by the time we approached the lone pine with the thatching ants' hill at its side. The fruits on the golden currant bush remained tasty, if a bit past their prime. We were able to step right up and pick them because the ant mound, which had swelled with a pulsating fury during my first encounter three months before, had somehow shrunk in size so much that for several minutes I thought we had come to the wrong place. At our feet, the great nest amounted to little more than a patch of scattered duff, with not a single ant in sight.

While I poked at the needle-strewn ground, trying to uncover a spark of activity, Dr. Hansen watched impassively. "What's going on?" I asked, looking to her for help. "Do they settle in for winter this early?"

She shook her head. "I guess some do, but there's more going on here than that. This mound has died. Ant colonies have a life span, just like anything else."

Stretching my arms out like the schoolgirl did in May, I tried to demonstrate how large the tumulus had been then.

"All that energy inside, all that work and movement, combine to puff their material way up," said Hansen. "If the colony is not alive, the duff flattens right back down. But don't take it personally. Next spring we can find as many new mounds as you want to puzzle over. I'm pretty sure thatching ants will be around long after we're gone."

The way it turned out, not more than a couple of weeks went by before a friend relayed a message to me from the Spokane Reservation. On a sandy bluff above the mouth of the river, she and her husband had found the biggest anthill anyone there had ever seen—as tall as a man and even larger across. The photograph they sent showed one of them standing next to it, holding up a walking stick for scale. Looking at that massive mound, it was hard not to compare it to a termite structure in Africa, one of those exotic hoodoos that Laurel Hansen used to dream about before she discovered an architecture just as interesting, much closer to home.

IX
THE WHOLE BAG
OF CRAYONS

Kaleidoscope

The thing about geology is that it never stops. "No causes whatever have . . . ever acted, but those that are now acting," wrote
the pioneering Scottish geologist Charles Lyell, "and they never
acted with different degrees of energy from that which they
now exert." According to Lyell's insight, the earth has always
turned, and will continue to turn, like a kaleidoscope of unfath-
omable scale. Massive floods will rearrange the landscape. Lava
flows will ooze from volcanic vents. Deeply buried ocean sediments will return to the surface in reconstituted form. Although
human existence spans only a tiny arc in the rotation of this
spinning time machine, Lyell asserted that an observant person
could make sense of all the constituents because the ongoing

processes have remained consistent. Visual clues lie in plain sight, like distinct glass shards that reappear in each new turn of the kaleidoscope.

Such clues are scattered across the Okanogan Highlands in what is now north central Washington State and adjacent British Columbia. Around a hundred million years ago, a crescent of volcanic islands that geologists call Quesnellia docked against primordial North America. During its initial contact, this terrane overrode the continental basement rock in a long slide that raised the elevation of the land between the Rockies and the Cascades several thousand feet above its present level. In effect, Quesnellia's overthrust thickened a portion of the earth's crust. It is a geological tenet that such disproportions tend to even out over time.

By the turn of the Eocene epoch, a fault beneath the margin of Quesnellia's collision extended to the earth's mantle. From that molten source, a batholith of magma filled the empty space, creating pressure and fractures within both the basement rock and the overthrust terrane. The magma funneled up through the cracks in a pulsating series of events known as the Sanpoil Volcanics, which left igneous flows puddled over the top of the Quesnellia formations. Further batholithic forces fractured both the new and old horizons into a series of tangled uplifts. As the pressure abated, the earth's crust was stretched and thinned. The more brittle upper crust cracked into fault blocks that slipped and slid against each other like books slumping across a loosely packed shelf. Depressions between the angled bookends filled with fresh water to form substantial lakes.

The timing of the Sanpoil Volcanics, a bit more than fifty million years ago, coincided with a warm, mild Eocene climate. After the geologic activity settled down, the conditions gave rise to a temperate upland forest around the edge of one lake that touched the site of the modern town of Republic, Washington. Similar forests, surrounding similar lakes, arose within the thickened edges of overthrust islands that extended north and west all the way to Smithers, British Columbia. These Eocene forests and lakes supported roses and witch hazel, palm beetles and salmon, songbirds and crawdads.

Species lived, died, and sank to the bottoms of the scattered high lakes for thousands of years. Light volcanic ashfall and seasonal flood events introduced sediments that covered the detritus with just the right delicate velocity to preserve leaf surfaces, flower buds, spider bodies, and the tracery of horsefly wings. Over longer spans of time, the weight of these sediment layers pressed the organic images into fossils of exquisite detail.

Then, as the kaleidoscope began to turn again, the crust below the Okanogan Highlands slowly settled into the rolling domes and faulted exposures we see today. Those long-buried lakes remained remarkably undisturbed by the variety of geologic events that continued to shape the region. Even after commercial miners arrived to explore for veins of precious ore that had flowed close to the surface during the Sanpoil Volcanics, many components of the temperate Eocene forest slumbered on in their mudstone beds—each one a bright shard from the distant past, waiting to be revealed.

Getting to Boot Hill

In the summer of 1977, a pair of volunteers from the University of Washington's Burke Museum crossed the North Cascades for a weekend fossil hunt in the Okanogan Highlands. Teenaged Kirk Johnson served as chauffeur for Wes Wehr, a self-taught paleo-botanist who, although he was pushing fifty, had never learned to drive. Their first target was Republic, a small gold-mining town where leaf fossils had been collected haphazardly since the late nineteenth century. Most experts had assumed the imprints were associated with Miocene leaf fossils found in clay beds farther south and had moved along to other sites.

Wehr and Johnson wandered along a drainage ditch across the street from Republic's city hall without finding anything and were close to getting back in the car when Johnson kicked a laminated rock. Before his foot had settled back to earth, the pair found themselves staring at the clear imprint of a dawn redwood twig. Soon they discovered several more troves of fossil-rich shales exposed by roadcuts and former mining digs along the base of a knobby outcrop called Boot Hill. It took a little longer to establish that what they had stumbled upon was not a Miocene forest of the sort they knew from the Columbia Basin, but rather the bed of a much older Eocene lake. For Johnson, that lucky kick helped to shape a paleontological path that led from Boot Hill to the Denver Museum of Nature and Science, and on to the Smithsonian Institution. For Wehr, already well along on a serendipitous life journey, the incident provided a focus that drew on all his eclectic qualities.

Wes Wehr had been born on the west side of the Cascades in 1929, and from an early age his precocious intelligence led him to pursue both classical music and concrete connections to the composers he adored. A letter-writing campaign brought him the autographs of Arnold Schoenberg, Dmitry Shostakovich, Jean Sibelius, and Igor Stravinsky. Always one to look beyond the obvious, Wehr then began to diversify his signature cache until it included blues progenitor W. C. Handy, Henri Matisse, George Bernard Shaw, and Albert Einstein. As a teenage usher at a popular Seattle theater, Wehr reveled in the thrill of interviewing luminaries ranging from Bela Lugosi to Paul Robeson for his high school newspaper. He learned when to linger in the shadows backstage, and when to make a decisive introduction.

Early on, Wehr's collecting bug extended to agates and unusual shells, which he connected to the kind of timeless beauty he always felt in the presence of fine art. "When I was young," he wrote later, "I had no inkling that in time I'd become a paleontologist. But everywhere I went I came upon traces of ancient life."

A pair of accomplished musical scores Wehr wrote in high school helped him gain entry to the University of Washington in 1947. Within two years he had won a fellowship for his original compositions. When one of his professors took a brief vacation, Wes—slight of frame, blue-eyed, full of enthusiasm, and not yet twenty years old—found himself teaching piano composition to Mark Tobey, by then pushing sixty and well established as a world art star. The two became lifelong friends, and Tobey introduced Wehr to Seattle's bohemian art scene. Tobey kept a piano wherever he lived, and always played his newest creations for Wehr; both men also shared an interest in natural artifacts and occasionally toured the mineral collections at the Burke Museum together.

Mark Tobey cultivated associates on a high level, and Wehr was never shy about tagging along. "Wes had this weird sense for famous people," one of his colleagues recalled. "I don't know why." Wehr developed a habit of scribbling down snippets of conversations with his eminent friends, and eventually used them as the raw material for a pair of memoirs.

When poet Elizabeth Bishop arrived in Seattle to teach writing classes, Wes sat in on her sessions and began another extended friendship. Around 1960, at a time when he was struggling with his musical career, he took up painting, creating tiny impressionistic landscapes with wax crayons. "I tried to paint landscapes that were like the mysterious vistas I saw in polished petrified wood from the Ginkgo Petrified Forest near Vantage, in eastern Washington," he explained. "Or like the 'landscapes' in polished thunder egg agates from the Oregon desert." Wehr carried his small works around in a battered briefcase and would whip them out to show friends in coffee shops around town. Elizabeth Bishop was charmed, and for Wehr's first exhibit in the mid-1960s, she contributed a gallery note praising the painter's "chilling sensation of time and space." In private, the poet made a point of telling Wes he needed to widen his scope of experience. Around the same time, Mark Tobey, who at first had also encouraged Wes's painting, offered a critique that Wehr recorded in one of his notebooks: "Your landscapes have a nice poetic quality. But I can't always tell how strong your artistic will is. . . . Maybe you need to go do something else for a while— maybe some rockhounding. Or go to the Oregon coast and collect some more agates. . . . That interest of yours in agates and fossils is going to save your neck in the long run, I predict!"

Wehr hardly needed encouragement along those lines. As a lark, he and a companion fired off a package to Hermann Hesse that contained profuse appreciation for his books, some petrified wood from eastern Washington, and a polished agate nodule from the Oregon desert: "This stone was called a 'thunder egg' by the early Indians," they explained to Hesse. The great author replied with a small book of reproductions of his own watercolor landscapes.

Wes also used ancient stones to build a relationship with the philosopher Susanne Langer, who in the 1940s and '50s produced rigorous but popular books focused on theories of art and seeing. Langer provided a wellspring not only of analytical thought but also of clear observation that could bridge artistic and intellectual boundaries. Wehr loved the fact that she always carried her cello with her wherever she traveled but still knew how to make a picnic for the field; when he visited Langer in New York State, they would comb famous trilobite sites for curios to take home. Like Tobey, Langer was almost four decades older than Wehr, and she wielded considerable influence on his mind.

"It's nearly impossible for me to figure out now just when and how I began to evolve toward becoming a paleobotanist," he wrote later.

> It was hardly a conscious decision. . . . My visits to the paleontology rooms of great museums introduced me to a world of endlessly fascinating rare minerals, crystals, fossils, and their extraordinary aesthetic beauty. My embryonic painter's eye responded to them. I began to want to know about how they were formed, about the geological times and environments in which they once lived, just as I now lived in my own time and place.
>
> I think it was Susanne Langer, with her insatiable interest in the scientific nature of things, combined with her naturalist's appreciation for the outdoors, who was the single most important personal influence in directing my life toward that of a paleontologist.

Throughout the 1960s and '70s, Wehr continued to ride into the wild with artist friends to explore the essence of things. Often their destination was the dry side of the Cascades, where they could search Crab Creek for petrified wood or climb talus slopes in Moses Coulee to peer into rock shelters. "In the desert at night," Wehr ruminated, "looking at the basalt cliffs and the full moon above them, I began to visualize what the landscape had once been. Those nights in the desert became meditations on how all things change: the landscape, human relationships, and the values that dominate one's life from season to season."

Curious about the formal geology that lay beneath these landscapes, he began to correspond with George Beck, a geology professor at Central Washington University in Ellensburg. Beck had begun exploring significant Miocene fossil sites in the Columbia Basin in 1925, and as a classical violinist, he also displayed the kind of artist's sensibility that appealed to Wehr. In 1934, Beck published the first major paper about a petrified forest exposed above the Columbia River crossing at Vantage. Over the next several years, he played a key role in establishing Gingko Petrified Forest State Park, which interpreted this fifteen-million-year-old environment for the general public. Wehr counted Beck as an important mentor and joined him for digs at Ginkgo and various other Miocene sites in Yakima Canyon.

Wehr also continued his artistic pursuits, experimenting with melted crayons to produce effects that could be compared to the way hot magma metamorphoses geologic strata. He made friends with Seattle artist Joseph Goldberg, who was advancing his own encaustic techniques. They were both interested in beautiful stones and together made several visits to eastern Washington and Oregon—not digging for fossils, but stopping at rock shops in search of high-grade agates and thunder eggs. The pair would line up all the moss agates in whatever new store they came across, then study the green-chrome or rusty-iron filigree traced across milky quartz fields and judge which one was aesthetically best. It was clear to Goldberg that Wehr had a very pure eye for both art and agates, and that he was a hell of a painter. He was disappointed when Wes began spending less time melting crayons and more time swinging a rock hammer.

Wehr himself did not see such a clear distinction between art and science. His correspondence with professional paleobotanists carried the same fervor that he applied to his artistic friends, and his sharp eye for detail served him well in his outdoor avocation. In 1976, the Burke Museum named Wes an affiliate curator of paleobotany. The post came without a salary, but it did provide Wehr with a small office space and gained him access to the Burke's extensive collections and network of researchers.

Several of those associates recognized the quality of Wehr's work and always seemed to come up with funds for proposed field trips. His journey to the Okanogan Highland town of Republic with Kirk Johnson was only one of many that bore fruit.

Environmental Solitude

In 1985, Wes Wehr dropped by Spokane's Cheney Cowles Museum to pitch an exhibit on the work of Helmi Juvonen, one of his many west-side artist friends. The response was favorable, and Wehr accepted an offer of modest funds for travel and loan arrangements. After Helmi passed away, Wehr pressed on with the project, procuring all the items for the exhibit. At the opening he gave a talk to patrons, and after the exhibit closed he arranged permanent donations of several of the artist's pieces to the museum.

Although Mark Tobey, the acknowledged flag bearer of the Northwest School of art, had died in Switzerland a decade previously, Wehr told the museum's curator that over the years he had presented Tobey with numerous rocks, fossils, and crystals that had influenced the master's art. Even now, he suggested, he had access to enough Tobey material to mount a second exhibit.

In 1988, Wes arranged for loans of several of Tobey's minerals and personal effects archived at the Burke Museum, then called on several private collectors to supply a variety of original graphic art for the exhibit. He juxtaposed these framed pieces with the Burke artifacts, set in clear vitrine boxes, in order to highlight their impact on Tobey's thinking. The artifacts included many of Wehr's personal favorites, from fine jasper and obsidian to fossil ocean shells to one butter-smooth fragment of a Chinese walnut tree that during the Miocene had flourished in Yakima Canyon.

A fossilized water fern, genus *Azolla*, hailed from Republic in the Okanogan Highlands. *Azolla*'s leafy stems were etched black on a buff-colored mudstone slab that dated back to the Eocene, fifty million years before the show, and somehow seemed to capture the best of Tobey's intentions. For much of the artist's career, Tobey would insist that his wildly abstract art dealt with the real world, reflecting his attempt to balance science and spirituality according to his understanding of the Baha'i faith. The comparisons in the exhibit allowed one local reviewer to take the artist's point to heart. "After viewing the patterns and designs in Tobey's collection of rocks and fossils," she wrote, "I can see what he means."

When the show closed, Wehr funneled several permanent donations of works by Tobey and associated Northwest School artists to the museum's nascent collection. A couple of them had been created by Wehr himself, whose own position in the Seattle art scene was based on his small land- and seascapes. As a second signature style, Wehr later executed black spidery figures that reminded some people of dendrites, those branching mineral stains that seep to life inside layers of stone.

In keeping with Wehr's preferred scale, these creatures were the size of postcards.

In 1991, the Spokane museum premiered another exhibit titled *Environmental Solitude*, which jointly displayed works by Wes Wehr and encaustic master Joseph Goldberg. At the opening, a reporter described Wehr as dressed like an academic; shy to the point of stammering yet eager to talk about both art and paleobotany; standing alone in a corner but cajoling anyone who entered his orbit to inscribe their contact information into his well-worn address book—Wes always said he'd like to stay in touch. In the interview, Wehr played down his artwork to focus on a fossil project he was involved in three hours north of Spokane. Ancient leaf imprints there had attracted the attention of an eminent British paleobotanist, who, by chance, was on hand to attend the exhibit premier. "The interesting thing for me tonight is that my life is divided between paleontology and painting, and that's a very good life," Wehr said. "Have a painting showing, take off tomorrow on a field trip . . ."

Even as Wehr was participating in exhibits at the Spokane museum during the 1980s and '90s, he was running back and forth between a host of isolated fossil sites—always on the move, always with a mission, always displaying an almost desperate need to show off pretty objects and to connect people with each other. The curator grew accustomed to receiving postcards announcing that Wes would arrive the next day on the bus from Republic. On these occasions, he never forgot to bring her a small fossil as a gift. She filed away dozens of his terse postcards and tiny stone imprints, but whenever she asked Wehr exactly what he was digging, he would answer curtly: "We found some stuff," or "It was very hot out there," or "I'm completely worn out." And that was about it.

"He never really told me much of what was going on up there," the curator recalled. "It was like a different world."

Names

All of Wes Wehr's paleontological cohorts acknowledge that his artful eye helped him clearly visualize the tightly compressed and often baffling figures etched into fossil-bearing stones. He had a way of recognizing significant lines, of reconstructing smashed features in his mind. As his interest in the discipline grew, he took the time to learn about analogous living flowers, developing his basic intuitive sense of what looked artistically interesting into an understanding of what, in the botanical scheme of things, might be significant.

During the 1980s Wehr showed some fossil conifer material to a professor at the University of Montana, and the two started working together, most specifically in Yakima Canyon. One of the slabs Wes passed along contained an undescribed extinct species of fossil fern, and his Montana cohort named it *Osmunda wehrii*. For the first time, Wes had his own name entered in the precisely ordered address book of life on earth.

Meanwhile, Wehr and a growing band of professional collectors continued to turn up new Eocene fossils at various locations around Republic. Along with a wide range of community members and a visionary city administrator, they decided they needed to share this bounty with the world, just as George Beck had with the Gingko forest. Their plan called for both a museum and a public digging site on Boot Hill that would be available simultaneously for serious scientific research, public education, and amateur enthusiasts.

As the concept took shape, Wes continued to crack fossil slabs at a furious rate. He also, for the first time, began to transform his copious notes into popular articles. One of his earliest publications laid out the promise of fossil plants at Republic and other Okanogan Highland sites. Wehr described how the middle Eocene epoch in these highlands had seen the rapid appearance and diversification of several significant groups of flowering plants, including roses, maples, saxifrages, heaths, and soapberries. "Today, 48–49 million years later," he wrote, "is a time for the similarly rapid appearance and diversification of many theories about their origins, botanical affinities, and geographical distributions."

To demonstrate, Wehr highlighted the Alabama snow-wreath, *Neviusia alabamensis*—a shrubby member of the rose family that exists today only in the southeastern United States. He noted that a pair of closely related genera grow exclusively in China and Japan, and that recently a new species of *Neviusia* had been described from California's Mount Shasta. "Indeed," Wes remarked, "this is a very strange distribution for a living plant!" The publication announced that a fossil species of the same genus, *Neviusia*, had been unearthed both at Republic and at a sister Eocene quarry across the border near Princeton, British Columbia. Obviously, untangling *Neviusia's* long-term life history would not be a simple task, but just as obviously, the Okanogan Highlands held information about it that was both important and intriguing. "Fossils from the vicinity of Republic, Washington, provide an important window to the Eocene flora and fauna of the Pacific Northwest," he wrote. "Paleobotanists have already recognized 210 species from these beds. Many of these fossil plants have been found only at Republic and are known from only one or two specimens. Moreover, species new both to the Republic flora and to science are still being discovered."

In 1986, Wehr was the second author on the Missoula professor's description of a new species of fossil fir tree found at Republic. Wehr also shared some of his finds with Jack Wolfe, a US Geological Survey paleobotanist based in Denver who was investigating what leaf patterns and forest diversity might have to say about the larger Eocene climate. Wehr's name appeared with Wolfe's on a significant 1987 US Geological Survey paper on the fossil plants of the Republic and Princeton sites. The report described how the outpouring of new fossils must hold clues to the ancient environment and geography, as well as the evolution and distribution, of several modern groups of temperate plants. The accompanying botanical list included more than a dozen new species that the investigators were obligated to name, and Wolfe and Wehr attacked this task with relish, honoring contributors both scientific and personal. The impact of Susanne Langer's writings and friendship on Wehr was acknowledged in a witch-hazel family relative that he dubbed *Langeria magnifica*.

Wolfe and Wehr's report brought new attention to the richness of the Okanogan Highland sites. Not long afterward, a pair of paleobotanists working at the Princeton quarry found a way to acknowledge that influence when they uncovered a preserved staminate flower that constituted a new genus. Connecting the amateur and professional team to posterity with a timeless pun, they dubbed their new genus *Wehrwolfea*. Such recognition provided great satisfaction to Wes. "On those gloomy days when I felt wraithlike and doubted that I even existed," he wrote, "I looked at pictures of *Wehrwolfea* in textbooks and erudite scientific journals. After that, what else could possibly happen to me in matters of art world 'recognition' that would ever be so exuberantly off-the-wall?"

In 1988, the Stonerose Interpretive Center was launched in Republic. There, exactly as Wehr and others had envisioned, students from local schools could join fossil enthusiasts from all over the world. At a reclaimed house downtown, visitors of every stripe signed in and picked up a basic set of tools. From there they trudged to a Boot Hill roadcut that exposed many layers of Eocene shale. Along this curving face, together they could crack open stone books to their hearts' content. Each participant was allowed to take home his or her favorite three fossil finds of the day unless local experts on the site determined that the discovery might be new or significant. In that case, the freshly revealed fossil remained at the interpretive center for a more rigorous scientific examination.

The Flowering

As most of the professionals who first published on the Okanogan Highlands drifted off to other scientific pursuits— there are always more fossil digs to discover—Wes Wehr continued to visit the Republic and Princeton sites on a regular basis. He was well aware that his instinctive return to the place followed the European Enlightenment tradition of scientific philosophers like Alexander von Humboldt and Johann Wolfgang von Goethe, who insisted that any understanding of the larger world required not only close examination of its smallest motes but also a steady awareness of their place in time. The seeker should keep detailed records of every movement, and spread them around as much as possible. Wehr learned early on that open distribution of such knowledge, like an ongoing Northwest potlatch, pushed everything forward, and he quoted von Humboldt himself on the subject: "To keep what you already have, you must always be giving it away."

Over the next decade, Wehr used his far-flung connections to help expand the potential of the Stonerose Interpretive Center. He produced a stream of academic and popular articles explaining what had been found and what lay on the horizon. These included papers about conifer, hardwood, flower, fruit, seed, bird feather, crayfish, and insect fossils that had emerged from Stonerose. He drew parallels between the ancient and modern landscapes, titling his compendium of the earliest known occurrence of several rose-family flowers and fruit trees "The Eocene Orchards and Gardens of Republic, Washington." He organized the latest discoveries into neat checklists of fossil plants and insects so that interested visitors could make sense of the imprints that they cracked out of the roadcut.

At Stonerose, Wehr also came into his own as a natural teacher, presiding over intensive fossil identification workshops through most of the 1990s. Sitting among an ever-increasing pile of split mudstone, he would project his laser gaze through a jeweler's loupe, grunting and muttering as the object in question unfolded in his mind. A former colleague commented that "Wes had a particular talent for inspiring interested adults and children alike, who would crowd around him at a shale exposure, enthralled by his ability to communicate his excitement for the Eocene world, urging that they, too, might make a contribution to paleontology." Wehr's odd charisma helped lure a parade of unlikely characters to the Okanogan Highlands, rock-splitters of every imaginable origin and age. If they were serious, he found some way to encourage each one. Years later, a student from one of those workshops remembered the way Wes had pointed out small details of leaf anatomy as they strolled through the University of Washington's arboretum. "You'll never figure this stuff out," he advised her, "unless you start your own herbarium." Wehr understood that placing present-day specimens beside their Eocene analogs, then making the comparison available to interested diggers, would elevate everyone's level of comprehension.

In many ways, Wehr always maintained the set habits of a slightly obsessive ten-year-old autograph collector. One of his many drivers described their epic road trips as a series of carefully modulated events. "We had to stop at every bakery, because Wes loved pastries, and in every tiny town, because he craved the way each post office would stamp his mail with their own postmark. Then when we got back in the car, Wes would hang his head out the window like a dog and just feel the air. Hang it out so far that you could watch his ears flap."

When *Washington Geology* dedicated its June 1996 issue to the fossil troves around Republic, the contents included, as expected, a pair of new contributions from Wehr. A separate piece by a different author, titled "Volcanic Arcs and Vegetation," began with a nod to its catalyst: "Many of us who were students of paleobotany during the mid-1980s vividly recall the appearance in 1987 of Wolfe and Wehr's partial monograph of the middle Eocene Republic flora." The issue explored the mysterious forces that were revealed when Wehr and Johnson kicked their first dawn redwood in Republic: the tectonic grind that created a vast and varied Eocene Interior Arc along the west front of the Rockies from British Columbia into northern Utah; the subtle interplay between elevation and temperature during the rise of the Okanogan Highland forests; the bursts of diversification visible in the fossil record that echo modern habitats in complex and often

deceptive ways; the myriad new and knotty avenues for study presented by the constantly expanding data set rising from the rubble
of all these precious outcrops; the irony of a modern world paying
attention to an unmistakably warm and entirely vibrant ecosys-
tem from the distant past even as the early twenty-first century
hurtles toward its own much warmer future with unsettling speed.

The river of scientific and popular publications continued
to flow, bouncing from Wehr's contribution in a 1998 Burke
Museum report to a 1999 *Smithsonian* magazine article describing how the institution's fossil arthropod curator was teaming
up with Denver's Kirk Johnson and a group of experienced
field-workers to assess insect damage on fossil plants from Boot
Hill. Wes Wehr, naturally, was coordinating the partnership.
"Over the past two decades, Wehr has brought legions of other
paleontologists to Republic," the article explained, "and taken
pieces of Republic to them."

As Wehr oversaw that lively exchange of people and material around the Okanogan Highland sites, he maintained his
many quirks. "I never saw him do one piece of laundry on his
own," recalled one friend. "He'd buy a bunch of clothes at
Goodwill, with a particular eye for good dress shirts of a certain
pale-blue color. He would wear a batch till they were falling
apart, then give them away at the bus station." Or as Wehr himself once put it, "I had two patron saints: Saint Francis of Assisi
and Saint Vincent de Paul. Saint Francis nourished my soul,
and the Saint Vincent de Paul thrift store provided my clothing." When an associate visited his office at the Burke Museum,
she noticed a hot plate, various cans of beans, a paperback collection of Flaubert stories, and several nice pale-blue dress shirts
on hangers. Among his possessions lay several small works from

Northwest School artists like Mark Tobey, handy and tradable for an infusion of necessary cash.

In November 2003, the Paleontological Society of America presented Wehr with their Harrel L. Strimple Award, which recognizes outstanding achievement in the field by an amateur. Over two hundred friends, including artists, musicians, writers, museum curators, librarians, students, and paleontologists, attended a party in his honor the night before the awards ceremony. Kirk Johnson, praising the presentation, remarked: "It is with true pride and deep friendship that I represent the more than twenty-five paleontologists who wrote letters in support of this nomination. Wes Wehr is a regional treasure."

The following spring, Wehr began planning a large seventy-fifth birthday party for himself at the Nordic Heritage Museum in Seattle. A week ahead of time he was calling friends to tell them all about the details of who would sit where for the shindig. "This was vintage Wes. The only time I went head up with him was over arrangements at a dinner table," said one of them. "He'd blow into a restaurant with a whole crowd of people, then insist on choosing who would be placed next to whom. In his mind there was a definite seating arrangement that would connect certain people and catalyze alliances."

When Wes Wehr died of a heart attack five days before his birthday, a couple hundred of his close associates gathered at the intended birthday party for a memorial service. Many who attended expressed surprise to see so many unfamiliar faces there, and to hear such different moving accounts of their connections with the deceased. During the course of the afternoon, most of the fossil plants that bore his name, like *Wehrwolfea striata*, cropped up in the conversation: two ferns, a maple, a fine brown lacewing, and a winged seed of unknown affiliation called *Pteronepelys wehrii*, "the winged stranger."

Lagerstätte

Today, the Okanogan Highland researchers who explore in Wehr's spirit think of their several known sites collectively: an arc of fragile lake beds, each one slightly different than the rest, that follows a line of rumpled terrain from Republic six hundred miles north-northwest to the Driftwood Canyon digs near Smithers, British Columbia. Taken together, they represent a far-reaching interconnected *lagerstätte*—a German term that defines a significant fossil site with exceptional preservation of a diverse suite of organisms.

These Okanogan Highland fossils are not confined to any single situation. The climate that created them doesn't quite match the weather we think we know. The habitats they suggest refuse to fit into neat categories recognized by current ecologists. Yet the species that pour out of them, like Wehr himself, continue to provide a flood of tantalizing information: full of names and new directions, contradictions and unsolved mysteries. There are unidentified bird feathers, waiting to take wing. Nine new bulldog ant species have been named, belonging to four genera, and one of those recurs at an Eocene site in Denmark. There are fossil palm beetles, which allow climatologists to gauge winter temperatures during the heat wave of the early Eocene, when those bulldog ants tracked across whole continents.

Most recently, in the northernmost of those ancient lakes, bits of two different Eocene mammals have emerged. One is the lower right jawbone of a tapir relative that must have been about the size of a cocker spaniel. The other is the upper maxilla of a tiny forest-dwelling hedgehog whose entire body was probably no larger than the collector's thumb. It must have taken an eye as alert as Wes Wehr's to spot it among the rubble, and to see right away how it might fit into the larger tapestry of the lakes.

Even as such discoveries pour in, Wes Wehr's presence suffuses Stonerose and its associated fossil sites, especially in the energy that swirls around the collectors. It's as if he remains fixed on the floor of the quarry, surrounded by fragments named by or after him, peering at an especially puzzling one through his well-worn jeweler's loupe. He holds the surface of the stone in question up to the light, looking like a little Cyclops, single-eyed and blind to many things, but acutely attuned to many others. As he once wrote, "These artifacts of eons ago were constant reminders that no matter how immediate the present might seem to me, it was only a flickering instant in the ongoing continuum and flux of all things great and small."

Several years after his memorial service, one of Wes's former office mates and some of her Burke Museum associates assembled a small tribute to him inside a desk-sized glass case, then placed it between the entry lobby and exhibit halls at the museum. The left side of the case holds an array of perfect fossils that Wehr collected, including a few samples from Stonerose. To their right lie five of his brightly colored rock-shop purchases, including azurite and amethyst—a small taste of the kaleidoscopic treasures that his fingers had caressed. Beside these, three flashy mineral crystals rest on a ragged swatch of cloth that Wes had always claimed was a piece of Mark Tobey's bathrobe.

Wehr's two hardback volumes of memoirs, full of dish on famous people and extinct Latin species designations, are propped upright on the other side of the case.

Beside the books, a photograph of Wes in Switzerland, with Mark Tobey and his long-term partner, fronts a small 1944 Tobey drypoint titled *Agate World*. Its lines seem to travel at a furious pace, like the paths of subatomic particles, quickly bouncing a visitor's eye to a sample of untrimmed agate cooked into a complexity of textures and colors by the earth's unending geologic processes.

One of Wes Wehr's seascape miniatures lurks in the back center of the display. Four polished moss agates, cut into perfect rectangles of ascending size, flow away from the painting. The artist's melted-wax creation reflects the shape, color, and tone of the agates perfectly, bringing to mind another memory from a friend who once helped Wehr move his possessions from one office to another at the Burke. As they were unpacking boxes, he suddenly presented her with a clear plastic ziplock bag filled with green Crayola crayons. Not sure how to interpret such a gift, she stared blankly at Wehr. He held up the bag, mumbled something unintelligible, then finally explained: "I don't use green."

X

Restless Earth

Two Casualties

Ann McCrae worked for some time in the archives of the Spokane tribe. She had terrific language skills and often could be found wearing headphones in front of her computer, transcribing oral accounts recorded decades ago by Salish-speaking Spokane elders. The younger generation of these informants included Ann's mother, Nancy Flett, as well as a group of her friends who spoke the language known as Spokane Salish. Most of these women and men had grown up in very traditional families.

As an occasional visitor to the nearby tribal school, I often worked with students on projects that involved language questions—a plant, a place, a family name no one could quite nail down. The answer sometimes lay within the cross-referenced categories and extensive genealogical charts that had grown out of Ann's transcriptions. She was very keen on sharing such information with the school, so when any of the queries drew a blank, she would call on interested old friends for help. The fact that such pursuits usually led to more questions only seemed to spur Ann on, in her own patient, quiet way.

One afternoon I visited the archival offices to find Ann standing in front of a whiteboard on her wall, looking perplexed as she stared at five cryptic lines of English and Salish text.

Born 1851
1872 Earthquake—21 years old
wch wi'chem
xs- ch- xʷ-
died Walla Walla 1904—53 years old

One of Ann's cohorts had copied the lines from a wooden grave marker in the cemetery of the Washington State Penitentiary in Walla Walla, almost two hundred miles to the south. Prison records identified the deceased man as a Spokane Indian. To Ann, the fading English letters on the marker made a very poor approximation of any Salish language sounds, but she thought they might match up with a story she recalled from one of the elders' audiotapes.

The story began before the Spokane Reservation was established and told of a young man who lived with his mother near the mouth of the Spokane River. They had been through plenty of hard times together there. He was about twenty years old when a big earthquake shook their campsite on a cold winter night. The strength of the quake terrified his mother so badly that she ran away into the hills. For days afterward, the earth kept trembling, and with every aftershock she would start running again.

Some neighbors finally found the woman draped over a fallen log, motionless. She never regained consciousness.

Everyone said that the mother's death hit her son very hard and filled him with anger. In time he took it out on somebody, so that he ended up in a prison on the coast. He stayed there for fifteen years before he was transferred to Walla Walla, and he died in the penitentiary there only a few years later.

"We'd like to know his real Indian name, something more than *wch wi'chem*," said Ann. "We'd like to identify him, and bring his remains back home. We have this one version of the story, but I think my mom's friend Sadie Boyd might have talked about him too—I just have to find out where. And I'd like to know more about this earthquake. Was it really such a powerful thing?"

The Shakes

In the late fall of 1872, much of the Interior Columbia District— that large portion of the drainage between the Cascades and the Rockies that had been ruled by the British fur trade system for half a century—was still adjusting to a traumatic shift toward American control. A significant number of Plateau tribal bands and leaders had refused to sign treaties with the United States in the mid-1850s, and the 1858 wars that followed those controversial agreements were still fresh in everyone's memory. Walla Walla, the Oregon Trail stop in Washington Territory's extreme southeast corner, remained the only interior town of any size. At the same time, gold strikes on the upper Columbia and middle Fraser Rivers continued to attract a steady flow of fortune hunters, and hopeful farmers bent on scratching out homesteads were spreading tentatively across the region.

As the weather began to clamp down that December, Indian Affairs agent W. P. Winans began his third year in northeastern Washington, based in the small settlement of Colville. In the midst of his chaotic duties, Winans posted a message to his Walla Walla headquarters describing an event that took place on December 14, 1872. His words soon appeared in a local newspaper.

> Our valley was visited by an earthquake at 10 1/2 o'clock P.M. The first shock lasted about three minutes, stopped clocks, shook down crockery and bottles from shelves, etc. Several slighter shocks occurred during the next five hours.
> The weather is cold, and sleighing good.

Winans's letter stands as one of several brief firsthand written accounts of the quake. Another missive, from Spokane Bridge—a new settlement just upstream from present-day Spokane—assured friends that four distinct tremors had hurt no one. "In fact, nobody around here had any clear conception of what was the matter until it was all over," the writer confided.

Overlapping reports from Umatilla and The Dalles, in Oregon, described between two and five heavy shocks around ten o'clock on the same night. In Yakima City, several cowboys had gathered at the Sagebrush Saloon to celebrate the end of their season's work when "there came a sound like some one hitting the side of the house with a flat board; then the building began to shake. The boys ran outside to see who was trying to turn the house over." Columbia River steamboat captain J. C. Ainsworth, aboard his vessel near the confluence of the Walla Walla and Columbia Rivers, noted that the event was followed by "five lighter shocks at intervals of about fifteen minutes, after which a heavy, rumbling sound was heard as distinctly as a heavy peal of thunder." Ainsworth considered the first shock violent enough to shake buildings and their contents up "pretty lively, yet no damage or injury was sustained by any one, that I am aware of."

The original tremor must have been pretty lively indeed, because people in towns as far east as Virginia City, Montana, and across the Rocky Mountains in Henry House, Alberta, also felt a succession of mild shocks. West of the Cascades, newspapers in the larger cities of Portland, Olympia, Tacoma, and Victoria all described a temblor, although questionable informants and overblown prose often left the strength of the disturbance unclear. These newspapers also ran fuzzy reports of stronger events in the Interior, including a landslide on the Columbia. Some said that it had blocked the entire river somewhere north of Wenatchee, emptying the channel below and forming a vast lake upstream.

Over the next few weeks and months, new accounts continued to appear. Purported eyewitnesses swore that several chimneys had twisted, and that a couple of cabins had been shaken to pieces. Rolling rocks had killed at least three people. Water on the lower Fraser River had jumped its banks. Mount Rainier had let off a smoke plume that blanketed eastern Washington, suffocating children with its sulfurous fumes. There was a report that "in the Spokane country the earth opened up and swallowed a number of Indians and their horses." Many of the wilder stories emanated from the vicinity of Lake Chelan, forty miles upstream on the Columbia from Wenatchee. These included cracked earth, geysers, waterspouts, rhythmic waves, and sulfur- or oil-tainted water near the lake's outlet. As years and then decades stretched out, anniversaries of the quake were marked with commemorative coverage that tended to embroider rather than illuminate the truth, so that over time a body of conflicting stories passed into local lore.

The event also piqued the interest of geologists, and a 1956 Canadian report attempted to sort through period newspaper accounts from Fraser River towns that included Chilliwack, Hope, Spences Bridge, and Quesnel. An eyewitness in Yale related "that violent shock of earthquake lasted 5 m[inutes]. All rushed out of the house-never so much alarmed in my life— dreadful sensation." The authors of the Canadian article postulated that the quake's epicenter had been located just north of the international border, on the west slope of the Cascade Range.

During the 1970s, as part of an attempt to determine the stability of several proposed sites for nuclear power plants, the Washington Public Power Supply System (WPPSS) commissioned a geologic study of the 1872 earthquake. The lead investigator on the WPPSS report was Howard A. Coombs, a respected geologist whose team did an exemplary job of correlating period newspaper reports and tribal stories with geologic evidence. Coombs's team weighed the reliability of each account, placing the highest value on the source's proximity to the most affected areas in place and time. They then applied their findings to the Modified Mercalli Intensity Scale of 1931.

The Mercalli scale, first developed in the late nineteenth century, uses oral and sensory evidence to determine the seismic power of an earthquake on an index of one to twelve. Level II, for example, includes wakened sleepers and clanking crockery of the sort witnessed in Colville by W. P. Winans. Level III on the scale referred to "motor cars" rocking in unison. There were no automobiles in 1872, but Coombs's team did find a clear statement that the steamer *North Pacific*, lying in the mud of a south Puget Sound low tide, had rolled at its berth and "creaked in every joint."

Both general fright and significant physical damage begin to appear at Mercalli level VI, and there were several reports of both along the east slope of the Cascades. A railroad survey crewman camped on a mountain lakeshore wrote that "in the Cascades west of the lake one whole peak was shaken off. Disturbance deep in the earth could be heard in its dull deep grinding which was terrifying to all who heard it." A Chinese placer miner, working a gold claim on the east side of the Columbia above Wenatchee, told a settler that as he slept on the bank above his stake that night, "the river rolled up on the land and the land rolled down to the river."

At the mouth of the Wenatchee River, clerk John McBride said that just before the initial tremor, he heard a powerful explosion that sounded like an artillery barrage. He and his partner were jolted out of their sleep, then thrown to the floor as they attempted to dress. The clerk ran to a nearby trading post, which had suffered extensive structural and roof damage, and while he was there he felt at least three strong aftershocks over the next hour.

Another cluster of interviews in which Coombs placed great stock came out of Chilliwack, a settlement on the lower Fraser River, and had been printed within a few days of the quake: "Houses commenced to oscillate; the earth rose like waves of the sea; the rivers splashed their banks." These kinds of motions meet the criteria for level VII on the Mercalli scale. Several of the difficult-to-verify stories from the vicinity of Lake Chelan, including reports of significant cracks opening in the ground and drastic changes in spring and well flow, match level VIII.

The Coombs report, published in 1976, compiled four volumes of information from around the region and then used the site data to assign Mercalli scale numbers to far-flung settlements around the Greater Northwest. While the report debunked many of the second- and thirdhand accounts that had appeared in newspapers from west-side cities, it left no doubt that a major earthquake had shaken an area that up to that point in time had been viewed as geologically stable. It also confirmed accounts from a variety of inhabitants that significant aftershocks had been felt across the region after the initial tremor and that "lighter shocks, forming many small fissures in the earth, were felt for several years in the surrounding mountains."

Coombs's team agreed with the earlier Canadian report that the quake's epicenter had been located on the west slope of the Cascades just above the international border, more than fifty miles north of Lake Chelan. The researchers assigned Mercalli level VIII to a circle around that epicenter, which extended east across the Cascade crest and south past Lake Chelan. The Mercalli levels in the concentric circles that grew away from the epicenter diminished like ripples across a pond.

Coombs and his associates estimated that the 1872 earthquake ranged in force between 7.0 and 7.3 on the Richter scale. They set the origin of the temblor between twenty-five and forty miles below the surface—still within the outer layer of the earth's crust, and relatively shallow by the standards of seismologists. Such origins create long, slow shock waves that often leave local buildings intact but can be amplified on unstable ground much farther away. Crustal quakes of this depth are often characterized by significant and long-lasting aftershocks.

The Coombs report was far from the last word on the 1872 quake, and a subsequent study, published three years later, arrived at somewhat different conclusions. Its authors postulated a 7.4 magnitude, deeper event that occurred in the mantle of the earth. They placed the epicenter around Ross Lake, just west of the Cascade crest but south of the Canadian border. Obviously, the wide range of eyewitness accounts coupled with a complete lack of instrumentation make it impossible to pinpoint exactly what took place on that cold December night.

On the Ground

The raw power of the 1872 event remains clearly visible at the landmark known today as Earthquake Point, twenty miles above Wenatchee on the Columbia River's west bank. The massive Ribbon Cliff looms directly above the point, and the earthquake unleashed a landslide from the formation that temporarily blocked the great river's flow. At one family encampment some miles below Earthquake Point, a woman told of walking down to the Columbia to dip out water for cooking on the morning after the quake. Upon arriving at her familiar spot, she was startled to find the entire riverbed dry.

Another story came from Wapato John, a headman of the Chelan-Entiat band who farmed and ran a store upstream from Ribbon Cliff. He described the river rising fifty feet overnight, flooding his fields and trading post. The next day the Columbia broke back through the temporary dam to send a scary pulse of fast water downstream. Many of the tribal stories were relayed through white settlers of the area, and many of those included expressions in Chinook jargon, which served as the common language of the time. One quotation was translated as "mad bulls down in the earth, these will kill all the Indians." Wapato John was said to have declared that "a bad Ta-man-na-was," or spirit, had set things off, and in response he proceeded to move his family off the Columbia and up to the east shore of Lake Chelan.

The cliffs above Earthquake Point are composed of massive pale-gray granites written through with dark ribbons formed by more recent volcanic intrusions. Viewed from close range, these lines of basalt carry a reddish-brown color that fits both their geologic origin and an Interior Salish creation story about a bad blind dog whose head was broken open by the sun. Searching for its den, the injured dog bled all over the cliffs, leaving behind many ribbons of dried blood.

Even though these gory intrusions make the sheer Ribbon Cliff look ripe for a cataclysmic event, recent geological investigations suggest that the river-blocking landslide of 1872 did not calve directly off its face. More likely, the earthquake triggered a release of colluvium, the unsorted rubble of soils, scree, and volcanic ash that had piled up for some thousands of years at the base of the cliff. According to this hypothesis, a sudden jolt sent untold tons of such debris sliding forward like an avalanche to impede the river's flow. Over a period of hours, the Columbia bored an opening back through the mix of loose materials, and relentless pressure from the untamed river quickly enlarged the initial stream into a torrent that matched Wapato John's description of a sudden pulse of water. Such an event would not leave many clues behind, but rock and tree-ring studies from around the cliff have revealed a complex history of other slides in the area, as if the bleeding dog had created a host of troubles over time.

A few miles north and west of Ribbon Cliff, a Pleistocene glacier pushed out of the Cascade Range to carve the very long, very deep gouge that today holds Lake Chelan. This glacier's terminal moraine created the dam that contains the lake, which now drains through the Chelan River's short, wild canyon to the Columbia. The size and depth of Lake Chelan seem to connect it to the spine of the entire continent. In 1899, an earthquake of 8.6 magnitude struck Yakutat Bay in Alaska. Only twenty minutes later, almost 1,400 miles away, a "volcanic upheaval" occurred on the surface of Lake Chelan, splashing petroglyphs on rock walls high above the normal lake level. Such violent sudden splashes or standing waves are known to geologists as "seiches." The Coombs report described Lake Chelan's 1899 seiche as "almost certain to have been earthquake-induced" and speculated that the 1872 temblor may also have been responsible for some unusual groundwater effects around the Chelan area.

Native accounts from the near vicinity tell of the earth subsiding up to five feet in one place, and of large cracks opening in the ground both at lake level and along a nearby hogback ridge. Some of the cracks released water that spurted two or three feet into the air and reeked with sulfurous fumes. One such gusher, which appeared in the middle of a tribal encampment at the lake's south end, ruined much of the people's stored winter food. The Coombs report noted that lake-bottom sediments near this site lay more than four hundred feet thick and that much of that material had been washed down from the trough's upper end, where natural copper deposits concentrated sulfide minerals. Shifts in that ancient mud combined with hydraulic pressure could have disrupted water patterns of the area and created small geysers that emitted stinky fumes.

Wapato John's son Peter, who was a teenager when the 1872 quake occurred, described a similar outburst below the outlet of Lake Chelan.

At Chelan Station a great hole opened in the
earth and a veritable geyser was thrown into the
air to a height of twenty or thirty feet. For weeks
the Indians from all parts of the country came
to see the strange phenomenon. . . . The geyser
continued all winter but got weaker and as time
went on it subsided. Springs in this location still
remain to show the place where there occurred
this remarkable water spout.

Today, just upstream from the confluence of the Chelan and
Columbia Rivers, a series of artesian springs follows the crease
between the slope of the glacial moraine and the extensive
floodplain that leads down to the placid waters of the dammed
Columbia. Initially diverted to irrigate an early orchard, for the
past century the steady artesian flow has supported a pair of fish
hatcheries. Known collectively as Beebe Springs, the upwellings
can be traced by a thick brow of Himalayan blackberry that runs
above the upper hatchery road for more than a quarter mile.

When I related Peter Wapato's geyser story to US
Geological Survey researcher Ralph Haugerud, he wondered if
the quake, in a smaller version of the action at Ribbon Cliff,
might have dislodged an avalanche of glacial till from the hillside to plug the whole Beebe Springs system. Aftershocks combined with the impediments could have created a geyser that
took months to settle back into a quieter flow pattern.

"Imagine a rubber hose filled with water and sand,"
explained Haugerud. "Hold one end up in the air. If you shake
the hose, your flow increases on the lower end. If you shake it
hard enough, it will spurt up like a geyser and stay that way for a
bit before pulsing back down."

In 2002 Haugerud teamed with three fellow geologists to reevaluate the 1872 event. Their method was to rigorously compare it with a dozen more scientifically documented earthquakes that had occurred both east and west of the Cascade Range in the twentieth century. The investigators concluded that the 1872 earthquake was probably a shallow crustal event with a magnitude of 6.8 and an epicenter east of the Cascade crest, close to the south shore of Lake Chelan. In an appendix, the authors also stated that their findings could not represent any kind of final word, because "analyses of historical earthquakes often depend critically on ambiguous descriptions of earthquake effects."

Gravy

More than a hundred river miles upstream on the Columbia and almost due east from Beebe Springs, between the mouth of the Sanpoil and Spokane Rivers, the prominent landmark of Whitestone Rock rises above the river's south shore. In 1872 John "Virginia Bill" Covington ran a store in the shadow of Whitestone. Covington, who was married to a Sanpoil woman known as Spillkeen, talked to a reporter in the spring of 1873.

> Mr. Covington, who has a trading post at White Stone . . . informs us that he spent the Winter in that country, and was there at the time of the earthquake last Fall. He says that he counted ONE HUNDRED AND FORTY-TWO DISTINCT SHOCKS continuing at irregular intervals for forty-two days. At one place he saw a crack in the surface of the earth which is now open for about one hundred and fifty yards in length, and is from two to three feet wide at the top, and is from two to six feet deep. At another

place he saw where the bank of the Columbia river had CAVED OFF AND SETTLED DOWN for two or three hundred yards. The mountains and cliffs were so shaken up and appear to be so greatly agitated and disturbed that large masses of rock are still constantly falling, tumbling and sliding down.

Succeeding subheads in the newspaper article announced both the appearance of "A BOILING LAKE" near the mouth of the Okanogan River and a "NATURAL BRIDGE" that formed over the Columbia just north of the Canadian border. Although the truth of such details remains impossible to verify, Howard Coombs and his cohorts did date discontinuities in nearby land-forms and confirm that sizeable landslides had occurred around the Whitestone trading post.

In the unsettled environment that existed throughout the Plateau tribal world in 1872, it is not surprising that a land-scape-altering earthquake would be seen as a significant spiritual event. The Okanogan-Lakes author Mourning Dove remarked that although many of her elders clung to their native beliefs during the missionary period that began in the 1840s, the shak-ing earth persuaded some to embrace Christianity. Even as the aftershocks continued, a frame church was constructed on the site of an original Jesuit mission just south of Kettle Falls. "During that time my people stayed close to the priests," Mourning Dove wrote. "The Black Robes [Jesuits] had no difficulty making life-long Colvile and Okanogan converts at that time."

The Jesuit priest Father Urban Grassi, who worked out of Yakima in the 1870s, interpreted the tremor as a sign from God, and in an 1874 letter commented about its effects on Sanpoil and Nespelem bands along the southern edge of the proposed Colville Reservation. Like Bill Covington, Father Grassi described significant aftershocks and landscape alterations, some of which score surprisingly high on the Mercalli scale for a place so far removed from the quake's epicenter.

> This tribe more than any other on the Columbia
> for the past two years has been visited by God
> with earthquakes that in some places has sunk
> the ground, in others has piled it up greatly, and
> in others has broken the sides of the mountains.
> At the sight of such terrors, it is something new
> that this tribe, like its neighbors . . . are begin-
> ning to fear and to pray, although the earth-
> quakes have not caused them to abandon their
> vices entirely . . .

If by "vices" Father Grassi meant traditional cultural practices, he was correct: many Native American people had their
own spiritual response to the upset of the earthquake. In 1873, an
Indian Affairs agent on the Columbia Plateau compiled a list of
no fewer than ten different native prophets or "dreamers" active
across the region, each with a number of followers, ranging from
a few dozen to several hundred. Two of these dreamer-prophets,
Smohalla, from the Wanapum tribe, and Skolaskin (also spelled
Kolaskin), of the Sanpoil, were said to have predicted the 1872
earthquake. A third, Patoi, of the Wenatchi, took advantage of
the tumult to increase his following.

Working a few decades after the event, anthropologist Verne
Ray gathered a host of different versions of Skolaskin's story. One
person told him that some weeks before December 14, 1872,
Skolaskin had ridden into the camp of a rival Okanogan prophet

and declared that "the Manitou is angry with the wickedness of his people. . . . The land is going to shake. Buildings will fall down. People will go out of their heads. You had better tell your people. Warn them as to what is going to happen."

Skolaskin and his party then departed for home. "All along the river they warned the people of the impending tragedy. They were laughed at by some, but many more took the prophecy seriously. Those who had become followers of Skolaskin began to pray to *qwrlantsu'tan* to deliver them from destruction."

After a day of travel, the group camped at the mouth of the Nespelem River. During the night they felt a slight tremor in the earth. As soon as they arrived at Whitestone Rock the following day, "Skolaskin gathered his followers together in the church to pray. Severe quakes occurred that night and throughout the following day. Further tremors were felt at intervals from that time until spring."

Julia Garry, a Spokane woman, confirmed at least some of the activities. "I was camping at Whitestone, not far from Skolaskin's camp, a little while after the big earthquake," she told Ray. "Suddenly one day Skolaskin rushed out of his lodge and called to the people to begin praying and to look out for what was to happen. A little while later another earthquake came, just a small one. More people believed in him after that."

Whether or not Skolaskin was purposely capitalizing on these aftershocks, for years afterward his influence remained strong. He ordered a small church built in his home village of Whitestone—one of the places most affected by the earthquake—and held regular services there. Skolaskin's Whitestone church was later dismantled and rebuilt in front of the main offices of the Colville Confederated Tribes at Nespelem, where

it stands today as a monument both to his work and to the reso-
nant power of the 1872 earthquake.

What Sadie Boyd Heard

Oral accounts passed down through generations continue to
provide sharp and significant evidence of the historic disrup-
tion. Coeur d'Alene member Cliff SiJohn grew up hearing how
an area around the mouth of the Spokane River sank during
that first night of violent tremors eight decades before. When
SiJohn's elders spoke the Salish word for the place, they would
hold their hands out, fingers spread and palms down, then shake
and lower them to mimic the effect. "That's what the word
means," SiJohn said. "All sunken down."

"I'll ask around about that word for 'sunken down,'" said
Ann McCrae, after digesting all the earthquake material I had
piled on her desk. "The Spokane is probably different than the
Coeur d'Alene. And the Kolaskin story is interesting. I don't
like to use the word 'prophet,' but I think he was a seer. Many of
our people long ago were seers. Some could see any time; others
could see when their animal or plant spirits guided them. In my
life I've known some, and have seen what they could do."

Ann handed me a file folder that contained a single page
of neat typing. She had found Sadie Boyd's recorded account
of the earthquake and transcribed it into English, highlighting
all the Salish names for people and places. Ann had tried to
trace out the site names, but she couldn't figure out all of them.
"Sadie was the oldest informant," she said. "Maybe the words
are old and those places are underwater now."

"Before I was born, and while my mother was pregnant with
my older sister, there was an earthquake," Sadie began. Ann
knew that Sadie was born in 1884, so the dates matched up well.

"There were families living at the flat above the mouth of the Spokane River, and at a place near there," Sadie continued. Ann said their second campsite had a name that sounded to her like "stuffed"—maybe it was a place where they gathered bedding, or stored food in pits.

"It was in the fall when the earthquake happened. The way my mother told it to me, it was so frightening that it made one woman lose her mind. This was Whist-m-la's mother." The son's name, Whist-m-la, looked similar to the name on the marker in the Walla Walla cemetery. But Sadie could not recall the name of his mother. Sadie said that the people at the camp "remembered Whist-m-las's mother running around, scared, and when it was all over they couldn't find her."

There were others, she said, who were just as disturbed by the earthquake. One man who lived at the mouth of the Spokane River kept chasing his horse, even though the animal was safe in a corral. But at least his family knew where he was.

Whist-m-la's mother remained lost, and it was only after a long time that someone found her body. It was in a place named for the sound of water, with rough breaks and steep side hills.

Sadie Boyd's mother told her how the trees and land were shaking and moving in the earthquake—not from side to side as Sadie had imagined it, but like boiling water, or something boiling. When Sadie grew up, she said she asked another elder who had been there what the earthquake looked like: "Did it shake from side to side?" The old lady said, "No. It was like something boiling."

Sadie Boyd also recorded the story of a separate seismic event that had taken place long before 1872, echoing the scientific analysis of the colluvium below Ribbon Cliff.

"It was awesome as it boiled like a giant pan of boiling gravy. Wave upon wave upon wave, fore and aft. People were running helter skelter, screaming, crying, as the land pulled apart, swallowing them up, swallowing the animals, trees, everything."

When I showed Sadie's Boyd's transcript to geologist Ralph Haugerud, he did not hesitate to interpret the account. "I immediately think of ground liquefaction," he said. "If you shake water-saturated sediments, they disaggregate and pack more closely. Then they release water, or muddy water, or sandy water, to boil up to the surface." Haugerud sent YouTube links of classic liquefaction from recent earthquakes in Japan, New Zealand, and Puget Sound to prove his point. Every one of them bubbled like thick gravy. "This is the kind of clue that we might be able to do something with," said Haugerud. "All we need is a few more."

From the scientific side, those clues will certainly keep coming. Haugerud's USGS colleague Brian Sherrod recently employed an aerial laser scanning process called LIDAR along the Columbia River south of Lake Chelan. He and several students with shovels then scrambled up to a suspicious spot in a tight canyon to expose a clear scarp—the kind of scar left behind when an earthquake ruptures the ground surface—that extends for three and a half miles. Sherrod thinks that geologists may finally be closing in on an exact source for the shadowy event known to some as "the earthquake that wouldn't stay put." That kind of significant news may hold ramifications for the way people live all over the Columbia Plateau.

I had one more story to share with Ann McCrae, told by a Sanpoil informant to Verne Ray in 1928.

An old man, Kapús, was looking for horses around Davenport. After he had found them he started back north, toward home. On the way he took a trail up a different canyon from that which he usually traveled.

Just about dusk, as he rounded a curve near the end of the canyon, he began to hear noises that he thought were ghosts. He looked over to a grove of cottonwoods and maples nearby and thought he saw a fire on the other side.

"Someone must be camping over there," he thought. He drove his horse over there, and when he rounded the bushes he saw a huge fire burning. There were no tents or horses, though, to show that anyone was camping there.

Then suddenly, on the other side of the fire he saw a woman with long, unbraided hair, wearing no clothes. All of a sudden the horses gave a snort and started running back where they had come from. . . . Kapús's horse ran also. None of them stopped until they reached the end of the canyon, two or three miles away.

The place where Kapús had seen the woman and the fire was an old winter camping site of the Spokane Indians. It had been deserted after the year of the earthquake. At that time an old woman had gone crazy from fright of the earthquake and had run wild through the woods, her hair coming unbraided and getting full of stickers. It was a week before she could be caught. She had died a while later.

It was the ghost of this woman that Kapús had seen at the fire.

"I read the paper you brought me," Ann McCrae said the next time I dropped by her office. "It reminds me how people then saw each other more and shared everything they had. San Poils and Spokanes had many kinship relations. They used to be down in Davenport all the time, digging roots, chasing horses. If Kapús wanted to drive them back across the river to the Colville Reservation, he could have taken any number of trails that run down on the Columbia between Whitestone Rock and the mouth of the Spokane.

"I don't know who that man Kapús was, but I will have a look. I don't know which canyon he might have been running his horses through, but I'm going to go back to that name in Sadie's story, the one that sounds like water lapping against the shore beneath rough breaks and steep side hills.

"I believe that Kapús did see the Spirit of Whist-m-la's mother. She might have needed to be seen by someone so that she could rest from the terror she went through that caused her death." That kind of terror, I think Ann was saying, could never be measured in numbers.

Coda
Skate Away

Winter is timeless, because the presence of ice can stop time's incessant flow. Not as often as it used to, of course—no one has seen the Columbia River's main stem frozen clear across for many decades now—but at some point after Thanksgiving, temperatures in the Inland Northwest usually tumble into single digits and remain there for a week or two. Clear ice skims farm ponds and flooded wetlands, and the skating season begins.

At first, I have to feel my way around artesian springs and fertile mud in order to remain on top of things. But if no warm wet system blows across the Cascades to push away the Arctic flow of air, whole bodies of water soon begin to turn over. Black ice can appear in some of the shallow flood-scoured lakes of the Columbia Basin overnight. Deeper glacial pocks to the north take longer, and the inevitable advent of snow lends a sense of urgency. Conditions at each site change from hour to hour, and it's easy to fall into the habit of sniffing the air first thing every morning to search for subtle clues. What might the ice look like today on one attractive lake down in the basin that my skates' blades have never touched?

To that end, I am thrashing through a wide band of bul-rushes that edge a secluded bay. The thermometer is stuck on zero and hasn't approached the melting point for a week. Last night's stiff west wind seems to have died down. From the high-way, the frozen surface showed wild patterns of darkness and light, but there must be some smooth ice out there somewhere.

I know this bay because white pelicans frequent it during the summer, but its wetland seems utterly different today. The rushes rise more than head-high, and the whole marsh is solid enough to walk on. I trace faint animal trails to the icy shore, where I discover that the breeze has freshened again. I stamp hard on frozen whiteness at the edge of the bay, then jump up and down. Not a single crack.

The surface a few yards farther along, although rough from puddled goose tracks, shines a little more clearly. I cross a series of jagged fault lines that allow me to gauge the thickness of this ice at something close to eight inches, which feels plenty safe. The greater question is whether to try this bumpy shore ice or to venture toward the unknown center. After a few tentative steps, two small people come into view across the bay, standing in the midst of several black dots. There is nothing like the sight of ice fishermen to give a hesitant skater confidence. Off comes my backpack, and I flop down to start drawing on the long laces.

Once I'm up, the ice immediately gets worse, forcing me to tiptoe across features that seem to mirror geologic actions of much greater proportion. Pressure ridges have buckled thick floes upward and dropped them down. Sheets of water must have exuded from these spreading tectonic cracks to flow across one another and freeze. One fractured intersection catches a skate and sends me skittering ahead.

Now I can see that the surface looks smoother around a teardrop island that rises near the lake's west end. This ragged plug of basalt carries enough height to redirect the wind. As I move toward it, I spot a third fisherman standing motionless in the island's lee. He has walked a long way across the ice.

The closer I get to the island, the more the situation changes. At first, I find that steady breezes have rippled recent puddle flows in exactly the way that tidal action griddles the sand on a hard-packed beach. It's better than the inshore ice, but skating over it at even a moderate pace still chatters my teeth.

Those ripples soon give way to a more extensive plain, where relentless wind has scoured surface-bubble clusters into a paisley pattern: curved ovals of frosted tinkling glass set into a dark ice netting. This strange terrain, I realize, is what I saw from the highway, and dominates the greater part of the lake surface in all directions. It turns out to be negotiable, and the trick to attacking it is to weave back and forth along the black net strings, feeling for their polished smoothness.

I pick up speed and close in on the island, shaped not all that long ago by successive Ice Age floods. Only a few miles beyond this lake, one of my favorite coulees yawns open in the scablands. From the center of that dry coulee, a flood-carved island very similar to the one I am now approaching rises like a fortress. As a memento to the ice time's dramatic end, the last passing deluge dropped a pendant bar of exotic gravel on the fortress's downstream side.

That bar and coulee look exactly the same today as they did in June of 1860, when a young Boston artist from the

International Boundary Commission climbed a terrace above the broad expanse of landscape to sketch the scene. He made a numbered key for the muted gray-green hues of the surrounding shrub-steppe, then daubed in colors aboard ship during his voyage back around Cape Horn. On the bottom edge of his work he wrote, "Aspen Camp, looking North. 27 Miles from Cow Creek."

The right edge of the painting curves along the bench where the artist had positioned himself, so that the aspen grove, fronted by a few tents, lies nestled in a cove far below. The basalt fortress takes center stage on the coulee floor, with a half circle of supply wagons stationed along the base of its pendant bar. The outfit's pack mules, released from their hauling duties, have scattered uphill from the wagons to forage for the night.

The artist had been working with a boundary survey crew on the forty-ninth parallel around the Purcell Trench when some of the axmen, charged with cutting a swath along the new international border, began to suffer from the loose teeth and aching lethargy that any mariner knew meant scurvy. "The Surgeon of the Escort advises that we send them to the Spokane River where there is a wild onion which grows along the bank which may prove of service," wrote one of the officers. That pendant bar, then and now, offers the kind of scoured ground rich in edible biscuitroots, while each May the wetter areas around the aspen grove still shine blue with camas lilies. The coulee itself sits in that in-between territory where Sahaptin ancestors of Mary Jim might have met Salish-speaking kin of William and Mattie Three Mountains as they all traced their annual rounds for roots. The land that had nourished these families for untold generations would cure the visitors' scurvy after just a few hearty meals.

Drawn by the winter lake's own version of a flood-carved fortress, I lean into my turns, veering away from the lone fisherman as I aim for wetlands along the western shore. Each fragile white paisley flower in the ice assumes a different size and shape, ready to send a skater flying, but the dark, hard surrounding ice provides a continuous cursive line to follow. I fight into the wind, pumping hard and slow, threading through an array of basalt boulders off the western head of the island. Turning down the protected side with the wind at my back, it's all speed now, and all I can do to keep my skates writing on the secure black track.

When I risk a glance up, I'm already at the island's east end, and I decide to duck under the protected brow of basalt rather than face a tough upwind return. The moment I round that rock corner, the solitary fisherman reappears. Given that this is the second time our paths have almost crossed, it only seems polite to pay him a visit.

The ice turns bad again around the foot of the island. Elemental forces have broken the surface into fist-sized geometric shapes and glued them together like pillow basalt, so that I have to stumble along at a painful rate. Without actually staring, the fisherman sneaks glances at my progress. I, on the other hand, have to come to a dead stop twenty feet away in order to size him up; otherwise, I'll fall flat on my face.

The man is short, squarely built, and appears to be a Russian. If so, he and his kin have a rich history in the Columbia Basin, ranging from homesteaders who began as Volga River farmers dispatched by Catherine the Great to a much more recent stream of settlers emanating from the splintered periphery of the Soviet Union. I think of one schoolboy I met recently who knew all about trapping and preparing pelts; in order to prove it, he had brought in a red fox-skin winter cap, complete with long earflaps, which a Ukrainian uncle had made for him.

From my tentative vantage point I can see that the lone fisherman's black wool cap has similar protective flaps, and that his body is wrapped in a quilted orange parka meant for a much larger man. Fearful that he might think I'm some kind of game warden, I smile and nod my head to put him at ease. He flinches just enough to keep me from catching his eye.

It takes longer to close that last short distance across the fragmented ice than it did to skate around the entire island, but once committed, I can't very well swerve away. I say hello at what I think is a comfortable distance, and feel the wind scatter all the sound. It is really whipping now, and I'm suddenly aware of the cold. There's nothing to do but edge my way along until I'm right beside the fisherman in the lee. I nod and smile again. He nods but doesn't smile.

"I hope my clumsy steps don't bother your fishing," I shout, wondering what could have drawn such a foreign arrangement of words from my mouth.

"Da," the man mutters. He is standing next to a hole in the ice, hands in his parka pockets. A heavy black spinning rod lies draped across the opening. It's impossible not to notice that although the hole was obviously hand-chopped through ice nearly fourteen inches thick, its circumference makes a tidy almost-perfect circle.

"Am I disturbing the fish?"

"Da." He does not seem annoyed and perhaps doesn't understand what I'm saying. There are two more holes nearby, each one hewn with skillful precision toward some ideal roundness. I point to the closest opening, spread my hands apart, and rotate them to form a tight circle. He nods, and looks at my skates.

"Having any luck?"

"Da," he answers, pointing to a tin pail beyond one of the holes.

I struggle over to the bucket and admire a nice catch of small trout. Beside the pail, there's a heavy short-handled ax propped against a battered tackle-box lid. The ax is pretty close in size and heft to the standard fur trade item that David Thompson offered to Plateau tribal people two centuries ago. There's something here, I think. This guy knows fish. He knows the tools of his trade. He knows his own version of the north country from the other side of the globe, and parts of it translate directly to the place where we are standing now.

I stalk back to the first hole in the hopes of sharing some of these parallel worlds. I nod, and the fisherman nods back.

I would like to find out how he got here, what forces spun him across the frozen taiga to land on a lake where he could chop such neat circular holes. I picture Odysseus, setting off to challenge an entirely unstable world. I wonder how to ask this man to tell me a story.

After a few more silent moments, I let a heavy gust of wind push me away from the trio of black holes. There's some ice nearby that looks close to skatable, and as things smooth out, I spot my shoes, waiting far across the bay. I venture a glance back at the fisherman as he tends his pole. Maybe if we meet out here again, the wind will not be blowing so hard. Then he might be able show me the way he tunnels down, through time and space, to reach the fish.

ACKNOWLEDGMENTS

This book would not have happened without the help and encouragement of these generous people and institutions.

Kathy Ahlenslager, Merle Andrew, Bruce Archibald, Steve Arno, Jim Baugh, Steve Box, Roy Breckenridge, Tom and Susan Bristol, Angela Buck and family, Pam Camp, Sharon Carroll, Francis Carson, Kay Comer, Jackie Cook, Helen and Win Cook, Chalk Courchane, Francis Culloyah, Jim Ellis, Ellen Ferguson, Pauline Flett, Ron Fox, Vi Frizell, Em Gale, Darlene Garcia, Dean Garwood, Joseph Goldberg, Charlie Gurche, Laurel Hansen, Jan Hartford, John Haugerud, Michael Holloman, Lindsey Howtopat, Larry Hufford, Gene Hunn, Tony Johnson, Gene Kiver, Phil Leinhart, Estella Leopold, Chris Loggers, Ruth Ludwin, Gary Luke and everyone at Sasquatch Books, Ann McCrae, Ben Mitchell, Pat Moses, Karen Myer, Wally Lee Parker, Madilane Perry, Kathleen Pigg, John Phillips, Richard Pugh, John Ross, Dick Scheuerman, Mark Schlessman, Beth Sellars, Brian Shovers, Darby Stapp and Northwest Anthropology, Michael Sternberg, Marsha Wynecoop, Tina and Judge Wynecoop, and Henry Zenk.

Asa Gray Herbaria, Harvard University, Cambridge, MA; Clayton/Deer Park Historical Society, Deer Park, WA; Eastern Washington Historical Society, Northwest Museum of Arts and Culture, Spokane, WA; Federal Records Center, Cheney, WA; Hudson's Bay Company Archives, Winnipeg, Manitoba; Loon Lake Historical Society, Loon Lake, WA; Montana Historical Society, Helena, MT; Multnomah County Historical Society,

Oregon City, OR; Spokane Public Library, Northwest Room, Spokane, WA; Spokane Tribal Preservation, Wellpinit, WA; Stevens County Historical Society, Colville, WA; Stonerose Interpretive Center, Republic, WA; and University of Oregon Library, Special Collections, Eugene, OR.

CHAPTER NOTES

Chapter 1: Chasing the Electric Fluid

p. 2: "as if to bid us good night": Thompson, *Writings*, Vol. 1, 126.

p. 2: "a Meteor of globular form" and related quotes: Ibid., 126–27.

p. 3: "phenomena that are peculiar": Ibid., 125.

p. 5: "We seemed to be in the centre" and related aurora borealis quotes: Ibid., 152–58.

p. 8: the global aurora . . . as a dynamic, undulating oval: Akasufu, 41–49.

p. 12: Kootenai elders: in Canada, the Kootenais are known as Ktunaxa First Nations People.

p. 12: one of David Thompson's maps: Thompson, *Map*, sheet 7.

Chapter 2: Meltdown

p. 17: "Spokane Natural Wonder Gives Free Ice on Hottest Day," *Spokane Daily Chronicle*, July 19, 1929, p. 1.

p. 18: layers of sage leaves: Ross, *Spokane Indians*, 436.

p. 19: reports about "ice caves": Halliday, *Caves of Washington*, 111–12.

p. 19: "cold air wells" in Thompson Falls: Dufresne, *A Heritage Remembered*, 203.

p. 20: A local geologist named Thomas Largé created a map: Largé, "Glaciation."

p. 21: Largé proposed that ripple marks: Largé, "Glacial Border."

p. 21: naturalist David Douglas and missionary Samuel Parker: Douglas, *Journal*, 208; Parker, *Journal*, 290.

p. 21: J. B. Leiberg postulated: Leiberg, "Bitterroot Forest Reserve," 256–57.

p. 21: Pardee visualized how this dam had impounded: Pardee, "Glacial Lake Missoula."

p. 21: Bretz published the first: Bretz, *Glacial Drainage*, 573–608.

p. 24: YouTube videos monitoring the removal of concrete dams: Howard, "Spectacular Time-Lapse Video."

p. 24: Some geologists contended: Waitt, *Case for Periodic, Colossal Jokulhlaups*, 1271–86.

p. 24: Breckinridge concluded that the bottom: Breckinridge, "An Overdeepened Glaciated Basin."

p. 27: One of Thompson's maps: Thompson, *Map*, sheet 7.

p. 28: "a range of Knowls to our Right": Thompson, "Journeys in the Spokane Country," 287.

p. 29: "all well, they have these 2 days caught many Trout": Ibid.

Chapter 3: The Longest Journey

p. 31: Early details and quotes from Ellis Hughes: Ward, "The Willamette Meteorite."; Pruett, "Ellis Hughes;" and Pruett, "Oregon Meteorites."

p. 32: a geologist exploring Oregon's southwest corner: Pruett, "Ellis Hughes."

p. 32: a fifteen-pound aerolite: Lange, "Oregon Meteorites," 106.

p. 33: their lodestone was owned: Fulton, "Oregon Iron & Steel Company."

p. 35: A. W. Miller—"a student of geology": "Searches for Meteor," *Morning Oregonian*, October 23, 1903, p. 7:1.

p. 36: "The 'meteor' was covered in sacks": "Contest for Oregon City Meteor," *Morning Oregonian*, October 28, 1903, p. 7:1.

p. 37: "the monster may have been buried": "Iron Lump A Meteor," *Morning Oregonian*, October 31, 1903, p. 4:1.

p. 37: Colonel Hawkins, of the Portland Free Museum: "Museum May Get It," *Morning Oregonian*, November 2, 1903, p. 10:3.

p. 38: "The taking and carrying away of all sorts of things": Ibid.

p. 39: famous Athens meteor: "Meteor Discovered Near Oregon City Larger Than Peary's Famous Find," *Morning Oregonian*, November 3, 1903, p. 4:2.

p. 39: "Clackamas Meteoric Iron": Kunz, "Clackamas Meteoric Iron," 107.

p. 40: "Napoleon of young American zoologists": Koch, "Henry A. Ward," Part 3, p. 2.

p. 41: "[Ward] is an enthusiast on the subject": "Deals in Meteors," *Morning Oregonian*, February 13, 1904, p. 9:1.

p. 41: a detailed description of the Oregon meteorite: Ward, "The Willamette Meteorite."

p. 41: The molecular structure: Buchwald, "Willamette, Oregon, U.S.A.," 1311–21.

p. 45: a massive fireball: "Forest City Meteor Caused Litigation," Greene Iowa Recorder, July 17, 1929, 13:1.

p. 45: a legal twist of his own: Pruett, "Ellis Hughes."

p. 46: "Ta-mah-no-us": Gibbs, *Dictionary of the Chinook Jargon*, 25.

p. 47: "The court found for the land owners": "Ellis Loses the Meteorite," *Morning Oregonian*, April 29, 1904, p. 4:1.

p. 47: "the meteor will be added to the collections:" "Hughes Will Appeal Meteor Case," *Morning Oregonian*, May 11, 1904, p. 12:3.

p. 47: they re-valued the meteorite: "Fell from Sky," *Morning Oregonian*, January 20, 1905, p. 4:1.

p. 49: "What is there to show that the Indians dug it?": "Oregon Iron Co. v. Hughes," *Pacific Reporter*, 47 Or 313, 82, p. 572.

p. 49: the Willamette Meteorite was unveiled: "Meteor Is Unveiled," *Morning Oregonian*, August 24, 1905, p. 10.

p. 51: "I have had a small piece cut from the Willamette meteorite": Pruett, Papers.

p. 53: a rough biography of the Willamette Meteorite: Buchwald, "Willamette, Oregon, U.S.A.," 1311–21.

p. 54: "The whole mass being corroded": "Oregon Iron Co. v. Hughes," *Pacific Reporter*, 47 Or 313, 82, p. 574.

p. 54: Willamette Meteorite "did not fall where found": "Cast of a Big Meteor," *Morning Oregonian*, March 29, 1908.

p. 55: Pugh postulated that the Willamette Meteorite originally plunged: Pugh, "Origin of the Willamette Meteorite."

p. 56: the Confederated Tribes of the Grande Ronde: Thompson, "Tribes Claim Willamette Meteorite."

p. 57: "It should have been kept here": "Cast of a Big Meteor," *Morning Oregonian*, March 29, 1908.

Chapter 4: A Taste for Roots

p. 61: Called "cha-pel-el" or "shapallel bread.": Moulton, *Journals*, vol. 5, 371–72.

p. 61: The word in Chinook jargon, *saplil*: Ibid.

p. 61: "a kind of biscuit": Ibid., vol. 6, 205.

p. 61: "2 pieces of Chapellel and Some roots": Ibid., vol. 7, 113.

p. 61: five dogs, along with hazelnuts, dried berries, and more root bread: Ibid., 118.

p. 61: "An umbelliferous plant": Phillips, *Plants*, 196.

p. 62: "The noise of their women pounding": Moulton, *Journals*, vol. 7, 239.

p. 62: "filled with horsebeef and mush of the bread of cows": Ibid.

p. 62: "The cows is a knobbed root": Ibid., 234.

p. 63: "about 6 bushels of the cows root": Ibid., 271–73.

p. 63: "We would make the men collect these roots themselves but there are several species of hemlock": Ibid., 275.

p. 63: "a parsel of roots and bread": Ibid., 275.

p. 64: "The Broken Arm gave Capt. C.": Ibid., 339.

p. 65: some botanists insist these two species cannot be separated in the field: Cronquist, *Intermountain Flora*, 414.

p. 65: The Okanagan Salish word for this deceptive plant: Turner, *Ethnobotany of the Okanagan-Colville Indians*, 68.

p. 66: The biscuitroots of the Columbia Plateau have adapted: Schlessmann, "Systematics of Tuberous Lomatiums," 16–17.

p. 69: Plant systematists who study *Lomatium* pollination: Schlessman, "Expression of Andromonoecy," 134.

p. 70: naturalist David Douglas: Douglas, *Journal*, 163.

p. 71: families living around the Yakama Reservation: Hunn, *Nch'I-Wana*, 99–109.

p. 72: "their horses were all in the plains with their womin gathering roots.": Moulton, *Journals*, vol. 7, 134.

p. 72: Mary Jim: "I am a Palouse Indian": Scheuerman, *Palouse Country*, 52.

p. 74: Little Sister and Doodlebug story: Flett, *s-qwellum't*, 8–11.

p. 75: "Indians tented off": Spokane House Journal, April 26, 1822.

p. 76: "The natives eat the tops" Pursh, *Flora*, 197.

p. 76: "*Umbelliferae*, perennial . . . the tender shoots" Douglas, *Journal*, 168.

p. 79: The Sahaptin man arched his fingers: Lindsey Howtopat, conversation with the author, May 23, 2013.

p. 80: "THE REAL INDIAN COUS": Henry Spalding, plant label, Gray Herbarium, Harvard University.

Chapter 5: A Possible Friend

p. 81: filed a Declaration of Intent: Naturalization Records, Idaho County, Idaho. Federal Records Center.

p. 81: returned to eastern Canada: Records, 1898-99, Ontario School of Practical Science. University of Toronto Archives.

p. 82: Manning was in charge of a large display: "The Mines at the Exposition." *Mining* 5 (January 1900): 4–11.

p. 82: traveling in northeast Washington in the company of a millionaire mine owner: "Local Brevities," *Bossburg Journal*, January 5, 1900, p. 1.

p. 82: in charge of thirty employees: "Local Brevities," *Bossburg Journal*, August 10, 1900, p. 1.

p. 82: locating and filing mining claims: Stevens County Quartz Records, Book 11, Washington State Archives, Eastern Regional Branch, Cheney.

p. 82: visited the superintendent of the Colville Indian Agency: Albert M. Anderson to W. A. Jones, 25 October 1900. Records of the Colville Indian Agency, Letters Sent. National Archives and Records Administration, Seattle.

p. 83: superintendent of three mines: "Local Briefs," *Kettle River Journal*, December 19, 1902; January 2 and June 5, 1903.

p. 83: reputation as a 'high flyer': "Local Briefs," *Kettle River Journal*, July 17, 1903, p. 1.

p. 83: Joseph presented Manning with a council pipe . . . and subsequent artifact quotations: W. M. Manning Collection Registry, Eastern Washington Historical Society, Spokane.

p. 86: "The spear is pointed with bone": Douglas, *Journal*, 203.

p. 86: subsisted with the Columbia River salmon: Chance, *People of the Falls*, 10–13.

p. 87: employers at the Easter Sunday mine: "Easter Sunday Is Hibernated," *Kettle River Journal*, October 14, 1905, p. 1.

p. 87: signed on as deputy surveyor for Stevens County: "News at Home,"

Kettle River Journal, November 18, 1905, p. 1.

p. 88: "the wildest of all Indians": Sidney Waters to Commissioner of Indian Affairs, 26 June 1884. Records of the Washington Superintendency. National Archives and Records Administration, Seattle.

p. 88: "The old people that are blind": US Department of Interior, *Report*, 81.

p. 89: "his people in the Calispel valley are being abused": "Lo Finds A Friend," *Spokesman-Review*, May 28, 1895, p. 3:3.

p. 89: "Kalispel women traded briskly in trinkets and beadwork." Fahey, *Kalispel Indians*, 84.

p. 90: Kalispel elder Francis Cullooyah suggests: Francis Cullooyah, conversations with the author, March 2008.

p. 91: "I remember a guy brought in a saddle": Ibid.

p. 92: Jesuit priest traveled to the Pend Oreille Valley on Christmas Eve: "University Head Ministers to Indians at Midnight Mass," *Spokesman-Review*, January 1, 1913, p. 6:1.

p. 93: Manning appeared before a judge: Stevens County Naturalization Records, September, 1906, Washington State Archives, Eastern Regional Branch, Cheney.

p. 93: Manning successfully ran for the joint position: "Stevens County Republican Ticket," *Kettle River Journal*, September 8, 1906, p. 1.

p. 93: Manning's activities for fall: *Colville Examiner*.

p. 93: "the display window of the Stannus-Keller Hardware Company": *Colville Examiner*, August 22, 1906.

p. 94: "*Tle* means 'mountains'": Pauline Flett, conversations with the author, winter 2008.

p. 95: "always a head above everyone else": Ibid.

p. 95: At Deep Creek, blending traditional and modern practices: Ruby and Brown, *The Spokane Indians*, 188–89.

p. 95: "He told father and mother": "Life in the Spokane Country Fifty Years Ago." Lewis Papers, Box 1, Folder 33.

p. 96: distinctive rock in the river: Pauline Flett, conversations with the author, winter 2008.

p. 96: "Intelligent, serious, dignified and straight-forward": John M. Webster to Commissioner of Indian Affairs, 11 February 1907. Webster Papers.

p. 97: Mattie affixed her thumbprint: Colville Agency Records, April 1, 1911. Robert Ruby Papers, Box 1, Folder SI 16, Eastern Washington Historical Society, Spokane.

p. 99: "like most of the old full bloods": John M. Webster to Commissioner of Indian Affairs, 12 June 1911. Webster Papers.

p. 99: Three Mountains led a council meeting: "Indians Get on Trail of Dill," *Spokesman-Review*, March 1, 1916, p. 10:1.

p. 100: William Three Mountains the Younger died: "Chief Threemountain," *Spokesman-Review*, January 15, 1937.

p. 100: "W. M. Manning, who has loaned:" *Spokesman-Review*, September 16, 1916.

p. 101: "This loss of course is that of your institution": Manning to

William S. Lewis, 22 March 1927, Manning Papers.

p. 101: "The loss of valuable articles from this collection": William S. Lewis to A. G. Avery, 23 March 1927, Manning Papers.

p. 101: an advisor for the mining division of the War Production Board: "Manning Returns," *Helena Independent Record*, May 15, 1942.

p. 101: felled by a stroke: "William M. Manning Dies Sunday in Bozeman Hospital," *Helena Independent Record*, April 2, 1945.

p. 104: "We will move on": Michael Holloman, conversation with the author, February 2008.

Chapter 6: Riding the High Wire

p. 107: He was every bit of thirty-three years old: Watson, *Lives Lived*, vol. 3, 891.

p. 107: "would have to be provided for in better shape": "Antoine Plante, Mountain Man," *Spokesman-Review*, December 10, 1933.

p. 109: "venerable lady": Steele, *An Illustrated History*, 202.

p. 110: The young farm girl would listen: Helen Cook, *Time Ticks On*, 4.

p. 113: "Stensgar dolomite": Campbell, *Geology of the Magnesite Belt*, 13–16.

p. 115: 1902 Washington Geological Survey report: Landes, *Non-Metalliferous Resources*.

p. 119: Northwest Magnesite: Buchanan, *Magnsite Mining*; Campbell, *Geology of the Magnesite Belt*, 36–46.

p. 117: Byron Riblet: Fahey, "Brothers Riblet."; Wells, *Tramway Titan*.

Chapter 7: Terra-cotta Man

p. 125: Besano fossils: UNESCO, "Monte San Giorgio."

p. 126: mixed hardwood forest: Robinson, "Stratigraphy and Sedimentology."

p. 127: state geologist visited the A. B. Pit: Glover, *Clays and Shales*, 287–89.

p. 128: Battista Giovanni Ponfatto obituary: *Colville Statesman-Examiner*, May 29, 1909.

p. 134: Leno and his friend Burton Stewart: Chuck Stewart, correspondence with the author, 2002.

p. 136: "At the plant in Clayton I learned to work": "He Won't Sell His Paintings," *Spokesman-Review*, December 7, 1958.

p. 137: "I'm no artist": Millier, Arthur. "Uncivilized 'Civilization' Depicts World Turmoil." *Los Angeles Times*, March 8, 1942.

p. 138: Leno as constant entertainment: Chuck Stewart, correspondence with the author, 2002.

p. 140: Children of all ages: Karen Meyer, conversation with the author, February 2002.

p. 140: "I can paint them without half trying": "He Won't Sell His Paintings," *Spokesman-Review*, December 7, 1958.

p. 142: "Leno Prestini may not be a trained artist: Ste. Marie, "Forward."

p. 143: Prestini's *From Clay to Clay* mural: Now owned by Loon Lake Historical Society, Loon Lake, WA.

p. 145: "Prestini could be a little tough to deal with": Neal Fosseen, conversation with the author, January 25, 2002.

Chapter 8: Sisters

p. 150: "That's what we call the thatching ants.": Klotz, *Urban Pest Management*, 40–41.

p. 153: "Birds singing, the pizmire, flies, beetles, in motion": Moulton, *Journals*, vol. 7, 192.

p. 153: "its stomach was gorged with winged ants." Lord, *A Naturalist*, 160.

p. 154: As the alates began to fly: Hansen, *Carpenter Ants*, 102–105.

p. 154: "Ant Time": Hölldobbler, *Journey to the Ants*, 11–12.

p. 156: carpenter ants proved to be a good subject: Hansen, *Carpenter Ants*.

p. 158: "nozzle jockeys": Klotz, *Urban Pest Management*, 1–10.

p. 160: Researchers termed it a "super-colony": McIver, "A Supercolony," 18–29.

p. 162: "Ant tightened his belt in order to bury the dead": Boas, *Kutenai Tales*, 213.

Chapter 9: The Whole Bag of Crayons

p. 167: "No causes whatever have . . . ever acted": Lyell vol. 1, 153.

p. 168: Sanpoil Volcanics: Steve Box, USGS, conversations with the author, 2013.

p. 170: the clear imprint of a dawn redwood twig: Johnson, *Cruisin'*, 3.

p. 171: He learned when to linger in the shadows: Wehr, *Accidental Collector*, 9–10, 222–23.

p. 171: "everywhere I went I came upon traces": Ibid., 34.

p. 171: "weird sense for famous people": Kathleen Pigg, conversation with the author, February 2013.

p. 172: "I tried to paint landscapes": Wehr, *Accidental Collector*, 81.

p. 172: "chilling sensation of time and space": Ibid., 49.

p. 172: "go to the Oregon coast and collect some more agates": Wehr, *Eighth Lively Art*, 30.

p. 173: "Susanne Langer, with her insatiable interest": Wehr, *Accidental Collector*, 117.

p. 174: began to correspond with George Beck": Ibid., 104.

p. 174: Wehr had a very pure eye: Joseph Goldberg, conversation with the author, March 25, 2013.

p. 175: associates recognized the quality of Wehr's work: Ellen Ferguson, conversation with the author, June 13, 2013.

p. 175: Wehr told the museum's curator: Beth Sellars, conversation with the author, February 18, 2013.

p. 176: "After viewing the patterns and designs": Kathy Brainard Cook, "Exhibit offers 'New Look' at artist Mark Tobey," *Spokesman-Review*, March 6, 1988, p. C-10.

p. 177: "The interesting thing for me tonight": Dan Webster, "Good Artists, Good Friends," *Spokesman-Review*, September 19, 1991.

p. 178: "He never really told me much": Beth Sellars, conversation with the author, March 3, 2013.

p. 178: his Montana cohort named it *Osmunda wehrii*: Miller, "Osmundia wehrii."

p. 179: "a time for the similarly rapid appearance": Wehr, "Eocene Orchards," 13–14.

p. 179: "Fossils from the vicinity of Republic": Wehr, "Paleobotanical Significance," 25.

p. 180: new species of fossil fir tree: Schorn, *Abies milleri*, 1–7.

p. 180: significant 1987 US Geological Survey paper: Wolfe and Wehr, *Middle Eocene Dicotyledonous Plants*.

p. 181: "so exuberantly off-the-wall?" Wehr, *Accidental Collector*, 197.

p. 181: Stonerose Interpretive Center was launched: Perry, *Brief History*, 44.

p. 182: "you must always be giving it away": Wehr, *Eighth Lively Art*, 199.

p. 183: "You'll never figure this stuff out": Jan Hartford, conversation with the author, February 2013.

p. 183: "you could watch his ears flap." Ibid.

p. 183: "students of paleobotany": Myers, "Volcanic Arcs."

p. 184: "brought legions of other paleontologists to Republic": Cannon, "Stories," 31.

p. 184: "I had two patron saints": Wehr, *Accidental Collector*, 72.

p. 184: office at the Burke Museum: Kathleen Pigg, conversations with the author, 2013.

p. 185: "It is with true pride": Kirk Johnson, "Presentation of the Harrell L. Stimple Award of the Paleontological Society to Wesley C. Wehr." *Journal of Paleontology* 78 (July 2004): 822.

p. 185: "This was vintage Wes": Jan Hartford, conversation with the author, February 2013.

p. 186: interconnected *lagerstätte*: Archibald, "Early Eocene Lagerstatten," 158.

p. 186: Nine new bulldog ant species: Archibald, "Bulldog Ants."

p. 186: fossil palm beetles: Archibald, "Fossil Palm Beetles."

p. 186: bits of two different Eocene mammals: Eberle, "Early Eocene Mammals."

p. 187: assembled a small tribute: Ellen Ferguson, conversation with the author, June 13, 2013.

p. 188: "I don't use green." Jan Hartford, conversation with the author, February 2013.

Chapter 10: Restless Earth

p. 191: "We'd like to know his real Indian name": Ann McCrae, conversations with the author, May 2010.

p. 192: "Our valley was visited by an earthquake": "Earthquake," *Walla Walla Union*, December 28, 1872, p. 3.

p. 192: four distinct tremors: "A Tremblor," *Walla Walla Statesman* December 21, 1872, p. 3.

p. 192: "a sound like someone hitting the side of a house": Splawn, *Ka-mi-akin*, 274.

p. 193: "no damage or injury was sustained by any one":"The First Shock," *Daily Oregonian*, December 16, 1872, p. 3.

p. 193: "in the Spokane country the earth opened up": *Walla Walla Union*, January 11, 1873.

p. 194: A 1956 Canadian report attempted to sort: Milne, "Seismic Activity."

p. 194: The lead investigator on the WPPSS report: Coombs, *Report*.

p. 195: "clerk John McBride said": Ibid.

p. 195: "Houses commenced to oscillate": "Chilliwack, B. C.," *Daily British Colonist*, Victoria B.C., December 17, 1872, p. 3.

p. 196: a subsequent study: Malone, *Attenuation Patterns*, 531–46.

p. 197: "a bad Ta-man-na-was," or spirit: Splawn, *Ka-mi-akin*, 329.

p. 198: an Interior Salish creation story: Layman, *Native River*, 80.

p. 198: recent geological investigations: Madole, *Ribbon Cliff*, 986–1002.

p. 199: ruined much of the people's stored winter food. Hackenmiller, *Wapato Heritage*, 89.

p. 200: "At Chelan Station a great hole opened": "Another Story of the Big Shake Which Dammed the Columbia," *Wenatchee World*, June 15, 1922, p. 5.

p. 200: "Imagine a rubber hose filled with water and sand": Ralph Haugerud, conversation with the author, April 10, 2013.

p. 201: "analyses of historical earthquakes": Bakun, "December 1872 Washington State Earthquake."

p. 201: "Mr. Covington, who has a trading post": "White Stone, Washington," *Walla Walla Union* March 15, 1873.

p. 202: "During that time my people stayed close to the priests": Mourning Dove, 152.

p. 203: "visited by God with earthquakes": Father Urban Grassi, S. J. to P. Giorda, S. J., 10 November 1874. Grassi Papers, Foley Library, Gonzaga University.

p. 203: Two of these dreamer-prophets: Ruby, *Dreamer Prophets*, 61.

p. 204: "The land is going to shake": Ray, "Kolaskin," 72.

p. 204: "I was camping at Whitestone": Ibid.

p. 205: "That's what the word means," SiJohn said.: Cliff SiJohn, conversations with the author, July and August 2006.

p. 206: "Did it shake from side to side?": Sadie Boyd. Transcript of audiotape by Ann McCrae, tribal elder, Spokane Tribal Preservation, Wellpinit, Washington.

p. 207: "I immediately think of ground liquefaction": Ralph Haugerud, conversation with the author, April 10, 2013.

p. 207: Liquefaction on YouTube: "Liquefaction video."

p. 207: those clues will certainly keep coming: Doughton, Sandi. "Scientists may be cracking mystery of big 1872 earthquake," *Seattle Times*, November 23, 2014.

p. 207: "the earthquake that wouldn't stay put": Ibid.

p. 208: "An old man, Kapús, was looking for horses": Ray, *Sanpoil Folktakes*, 183–84.

SELECTED BIBLIOGRAPHY

Akasofu, Syun-Ichi. *Aurora Borealis: The Amazing Northern Lights.* Anchorage: Alaska Geographic Society, Alaska Northwest Pub. Co., 1979.

Archibald, S. Bruce, Stefan P. Cover, and Corrie S. Moreau. "Bulldog Ants of the Eocene Okanagan Highlands and History of the Subfamily." *Annals of the Entomological Society of America* 99, no. 3 (May 2006): 487–523.

Archibald, S. Bruce, David R. Greenwood, Robin Y. Smith, Rolf W. Mathewes, and James F. Basinger. "Early Eocene Lagerstätten of the Okanagan Highlands (British Columbia and Washington State)." *Geoscience Canada* 38, no. 4 (Dec. 2011): 155–64.

Archibald, S. Bruce, Geoffrey E. Morse, David R. Greenwood, and Rolf W. Mathewes. "Fossil Palm Beetles Refine Upland Winter Temperatures in the Early Eocene Climatic Optimum." Abstract. *Proceedings of the National Academy of Sciences of the United States of America* (April 2014).

Archibald, S. Bruce, Kathleen B. Pigg, David R. Greenwood, Steven R. Manchester, Lisa Barksdale, Kirk R. Johnson, Michael Sternberg, Ruth A. Stockey, Melanie L. DeVore, and Gar W. Rothwell. "Wes Wehr Dedication." *Canadian Journal of Earth Sciences* 42 (2005): 115–17.

Bakun, William H., Ralph A. Haugerud, Margaret G. Hopper, and Ruth S. Ludwin. "The December 1872 Washington State Earthquake." *Bulletin of the Seismological Society of America* 92, no. 8 (Dec. 2002): 3239–58.

Boas, Franz. *Kutenai Tales.* Bureau of American Ethnology Bulletin 59. Washington DC: Smithsonian Institution, 1918.

Breckenridge, Roy M., and Kenneth F. Sprenke (1997). "An Overdeepened Glaciated Basin, Lake Pend Oreille, Northern Idaho." *Glacial Geology and Geomorphology.* http://boris.qub.ac.uk/ggg/.

Bretz, J. H. *Glacial Drainage on the Columbia Plateau.* The Geological Society of America Bulletin 34. 1923.

Buchanan J. E. "Magnesite Mining in Stevens County (1916-1968)." *The Pacific Northwesterner* 25, no. 3 (Summer 1981).

Buchwald, V. F. "Willamette, Oregon, U.S.A." In *Handbook of Iron Meteorites,* 1311–21. Tuscon and Berkeley: University of Arizona and University of California Press, 1975.

Campbell, Brian, and John S. Loofbourrow Jr. *Geology of the Magnesite Belt of Stevens County Washington.* Contributions to Economic Geology, Geological Survey Bulletin 1142-F. Washington DC: United States Government Printing Office, 1962.

Cannon, William. "Stories in Stone Read from Ancient Leaves." *Smithsonian Magazine*, June 1999, 30–33.

Chance, David. *People of the Falls*. Kettle Falls, WA: Kettle Falls Historical Center, 1986.

Cook, Helen. *Time Ticks On*. Colville, WA: Statesman-Examiner Press, 1990.

Coombs, Howard A. *Report of the Review Panel on the December 14, 1872 Earthquake*. Olympia: Washington Public Power Supply System, 1976.

Cronquist, Arthur, Noel H. Holmgren, Patricia K. Holmgren, and J. L. Reveal. *Intermountain Flora: Vascular Plants of the Intermountain West, U.S.A.* Vol. 3A. New York: New York Botanical Society, 1997.

Douglas, David. *Journal Kept by David Douglas During His Travels in North America*. London: William Wesley and Son, 1914.

Dufresne, Lorraine. *A Heritage Remembered: Early and Later Days in the History of Western Sanders County*. Thompson Falls, MT: Sanders County Ledger, 1976.

Eberle, Jaelyn J., Natalia Rybczynski, and David R. Greenwood. "Early Eocene Mammals from the Driftwood Creek Beds, Driftwood Canyon Provincial Park, Northern British Columbia." *Journal of Vertebrate Paleontology* 34, no. 4 (2014): 739–46.

Elliott, Charles B. *Practice at Trial and on Appeal*. Minneapolis: Keefe-Davidson Law Book Co., 1900.

Fahey, John. "The Brothers Riblet." *Spokane Magazine*, September 1980.

Fahey, John. *The Kalispel Indians*. Norman: University of Oklahoma Press, 1986.

Flett, Pauline, ed. *s-qwellum't': Spokane Legends*. Wellpinit, WA: Spokane Tribe of Indians, n.d.

Fulton, Ann. "Oregon Iron & Steel Company." *Oregon Encyclopedia*. http://www.oregonencyclopedia.org/.

Gass, Patrick. *The Journal of Patrick Gass of the Lewis and Clark Expedition*. Edited by Carol Lynn McGregor. Missoula: Mountain Press, 2010.

Glover, Sheldon L. *Clays and Shales of Washington*. Washington State Division of Geology Bulletin 24. Olympia, 1941.

Gibbs, George. *Dictionary of the Chinook Jargon, or, Trade Language of Oregon*. Reprint, New York: AMS Print, 1970.

Hackenmiller, Tom. *Wapato Heritage: The History of the Chelan and Entiat Indians*. Point Publishing, 1995.

Halliday, William R. *Caves of Washington*. Washington Department of Conservation, Division of Mines and Geology Information, Circular no. 40, 1963.

Hansen, Laurel D., and John H. Klotz. *Carpenter Ants of the United States and Canada*. Ithaca, NY: Comstock Publishing Associates, 2005.

Hitchcock, C. Leo, and Arthur Cronquist. *Flora of the Pacific Northwest: An Illustrated Manual.* Seattle: University of Washington Press, 1973.

Hölldobler, Bert, and Edward O. Wilson. *Journey to the Ants: A Story of Scientific Exploration.* Cambridge, MA: Harvard University Press, 1994.

Hovey, Otis Edmond. "The Willamette Meteor." *The American Museum Journal* 6, no. 3 (July 1906): 105–16.

Howard, Brian Clark. "Spectacular Time-Lapse Video of Historic Dam Removal." *National Geographic*, 2:01. Oct. 28, 2011. http://news.nationalgeographic. com/news/2011/10/111028-con-dit-dam-removal-vid-eo/?fb_ref=.TqwrTIW0q94. like;.Tqsc4PN9AvM.like&fb_source=home_oneline.

Hughes, Ellis. Interviewed by David Hunter and Betty Jane Thompson (Oregon State University students), 1938.

Hunn, Eugene S. *Nch'I-Wana: The Big River: Mid-Columbia Indians and Their Land.* Seattle: University of Washington Press, 1990.

Johnson, Kirk. *Cruisin' the Fossil Freeway: An Epoch Tale of a Scientist and an Artist on the Ultimate 5,000-Mile Paleo Road Trip.* Golden, CO: Fulcrum Press, 2007.

Klotz, John, Laurel Hansen, Herb Field, Michael Rust, David Oi, and Ken Kupfer. *Urban Pest Management of Ants in California.* Richmond: University of California Agriculture and Natural Resources, 2010.

Koch, Robert G. "Henry A. Ward," Pts. 1, 2, and 3. *Crooked Lake Review* 57 (Dec. 1992); 58 (Jan. 1993); 59 (Feb. 1993).

Kunz, George F. "Clackamas Meteoric Iron." *Science*, January 1904, 107–8.

Landes, Henry. *The Non-Metalliferous Resources of Washington.* Washington Geological Survey, Annual Report, 1902.

Lange. E. F. "Oregon Meteorites." *Oregon Historical Quarterly* 59, no. 2 (June 1958): 101–15.

Largé, Thomas. "Glaciation and Vulcanism in the Spokane Region." Paper presented to the American Institute of Mining and Metallurgical Engineering, Spokane, Washington, Nov. 4, 1921.

Largé, Thomas. "Glacial Border of Spokane." *Pan-American Geologists* vol 38 (Dec. 1922): 359–66.

Layman, William D. *Native River: The Columbia Remembered.* Pullman: Washington State University Press, 2002.

Leiberg, John B. "Bitterroot Forest Reserve." *Nineteenth Annual Report of the United States Geological Survey, Part V.* Washington, DC: Government Printing Office, 1899.

Lewis, William S. Papers. Eastern Washington Historical Society, Spokane.

"Liquefaction video of Japan Tohoku-Oki Earthquake in Central Park-Water pouring from cracks." Posted by faultbreak. YouTube video, 3:02. Mar. 28, 2011. http://www.youtube. com/watch?v=I3hJK1BoRak.

Lord, John Keast. *A Naturalist in British Columbia.* 2 vols. London: R. Bentley, 1866.

Lyell, K. *Life and Letters of Sir Charles Lyell.* London: John Murray, 1881.

Madole, Richard F., Robert L. Schuster, and Andrei M. Sarna-Wojcicki. *Ribbon Cliff Landslide, Washington, and the Earthquake of 14 December 1872.* Bulletin of the Seismological Society of America 38, no. 4. 1995.

Malone, S. D., and S. S. Bor. *Attenuation Patterns in the Pacific Northwest Based on Intensity Data and the Location of the 1872 North Cascades Earthquake.* Bulletin of the Seismological Society of America 69, no. 2. 1979.

Manning, William M. Collection and Papers. Eastern Washington Historical Society, Spokane.

McIver, James D., Torolf R. Torgersen, and Norman J. Cimon. "A Supercolony of the Thatch Ant *Formica obsuripes* in the Blue Mountains of Oregon." *Northwest Science* 71, no. 1 (1997): 18–29.

Miller, C. N., Jr. "Osmunda wehrii, a New Species Based on Petrified Rhizomes from the Miocene of Washington." *American Journal of Botany* 69, no. 1 (1982): 116–21.

Milne, W. G. "Seismic Activity in Canada West of the 113th Meridian, 1841-1951." *Canadian Dominion Observatory Publications* 18, no. 7. (1956).

Moulton, Gary E., ed. *The Journals of Lewis and Clark Expedition.* 12 vols. Lincoln: University of Nebraska Press, 1983–2001.

Mourning Dove. *Mourning Dove: A Salishan Autobiography.* Edited by Jay Miller. Lincoln: University of Nebraska Press, 1990.

Myers, Jeffrey A. "Volcanic Arcs and Vegetation." *Washington Geology* 24, no. 2 (June 1996): 37–39.

"Oregon Iron Co. vs Hughes." *Pacific Reporter* 81 (July 17, 1905): 572.

Pardee, J. T. "The Glacial Lake Missoula." *Journal of Geology* 18 (1910): 376–86.

Parker, Rev. Samuel. *Journal of an Exploring Tour beyond the Rocky Mountains in 1835.* Santa Barbara: The Narrative Press, 2001.

Perry, Madilane, and Lisa Barksdale. "A Brief History of the Stonerose Interpretive Center." *Washington Geology* 24, no. 2 (June 1996): 43–44.

Phillips, H. Wayne. *Plants of the Lewis and Clark Expedition.* Missoula, MT: Mountain Press Publishing Company, 2003.

Prestini, Battista. Unpublished memoir. Stevens County Historical Society, Colville, WA.

Prestini, Leno. Audio interview. Stevens County Historical Society, Colville, WA.

Pruett, J. Hugh. "Ellis Hughes: He Won Fame by Losing a Meteor." *Oregonian,* Oct. 23, 1938.

Pruett, J. H. "Oregon Meteorites." Unpublished manuscript. University of Oregon Library Special Collections, Eugene.

Pruett, J. H. Papers. University of Oregon Library Special Collections, Eugene.

Pugh, Richard N. "Origin of the Willamette Meteorite: An Alternate Hypothesis." *Oregon Geology* 48, no. 7 (July 1986): 79–85.

Pursh, Frederick. *Flora Americae Septentrionalis*. London: White, Cochrane, and Co., 1814.

Ray, Verne. "Sanpoil Folk Tales." *Journal of American Folklore* 46, no. 180 (Apr.–June 1933): 183–84.

Ray, Verne. "Kolaskin and the Earthquake at Whitestone Rock," *American Anthropologist* 38 (1936): 67–75.

Robinson, John D. "Stratigraphy and Sedimentology of the Latah Formation Spokane County." Master's thesis, Eastern Washington University, 1991.

Ross, John Alan. *The Spokane Indians*. Spokane: Michael J. Ross, 2011.

Ruby, Robert H., and John A. Brown. *Dreamer-Prophets of the Columbia Plateau: Smohalla and Skolaskin*. Norman: University of Oklahoma Press, 2002.

Ruby, Robert H., and John A. Brown. *The Spokane Indians: Children of the Sun*. Norman: University of Oklahoma Press, 2006.

Savage, Carleton N. *Geologic History of Pend Oreille Lake Region in North Idaho*. Moscow: Idaho Bureau of Mines and Geology, 1965.

Schlessman, Mark A. "Expression of Andromonoecy and Pollination of Tuberous Lomatiums." *Systematic Botany* 7 (1982): 134–49.

Schlessman, Mark A. "Systematics of Tuberous Lomatiums (Umbelliferae)." *The American Society of Plant Taxonomists, Systematic Botany Monographs* 4 (1984).

Scheurrmann, Richard. *Palouse Country: Oral History Edition*. Colfax, WA: The McGregor Company, 1994.

Schorn, H. E. and Wehr, W. C. *Abies milleri, sp. nov., the middle Eocene Klondike Mountain Formation, Republic, Ferry Country, Washington*. Seattle: Thomas Burke Memorial Washington State Museum, 1986.

Splawn, A. J. *Ka-mi-akin, the Last Hero of the Yakamas*. Portland: Kilham Press, 1917.

Spokane House Journal 1822-23. Hudson's Bay Company Archives, Winnipeg, MB.

Sowa, Tom. "A Tortured Artist Rescued in Time." *Spokesman-Review*, September 6, 1981.

Ste. Marie, Rev. Louis. Forward to Crosby Library of Gonzaga University's Leno Prestini Exhibit, Catalog, November 1960.

Steele, Richard F. *An Illustrated History of Stevens, Ferry, Okanogan and Chelan Counties, State of Washington*. Spokane: Western Historical Publishing Company, 1904.

Thompson, Courtenay. "Tribes Claim Willamette Meteorite." *Oregonian*, November 17, 1999.

Thompson, David. Notebooks. David Thompson Collection, Provincial Archives of Ontario, Toronto.

Thompson, David. *Map of North America from 84° West*. 1826. The National Archives, Kew, England.

Thompson, David. "David Thompson's Journeys in the Spokane Country." Edited by T. C. Elliott. *Washington Historical Quarterly* 9 (1918): 284–87.

Thompson, David. *Columbia Journals*. Edited by Barbara Belyea. Montreal: McGill-Queen's University Press, 1994.

Thompson, David. *The Writings of David Thompson*. Vol. 1, *The Travels*. 1850 version. Edited by William E. Moreau. Montreal and Kingston: McGill-Queen's University Press, 2009.

Turner, Nancy J., Randy Bouchard, and Dorothy I. D. Kennedy. *Ethnobotany of the Okanagan-Colville Indians of British Columbia and Washington*. Occasional Papers of the British Columbia Provincial Museum 21. Victoria: British Columbia Provincial Museum, 1980.

Turner, Nancy J., L. C. Thompson, M. T. Thompson, and A. Z. York. *Thompson Ethnobotany: Knowledge and Usage of Plants by the Thompson Indians of British Columbia*. Memoir 3. Victoria: Royal British Columbia Museum, 1990.

UNESCO. "Monte San Giorgio." http://whc.unesco.org/en/list/1090.

US Department of the Interior. Office of Indian Affairs. *Report of Coeur d'Alene Indian Commission, appointed March 2, 1889*. 51st Cong., 1st sess., Senate Exec. Doc. No. 14 (Washington, D. C., 1889).

Waitt, R. B., Jr. *Case for Periodic, Colossal Jokulhlaups from Pleistocene Glacial Lake Missoula*. The Geological Society of America Bulletin 96. 1985.

Waitt, R. B., Jr., and R. M. Thorson. "The Cordilleran Ice Sheet in Washington, Idaho, and Montana." *The Late Pleistocene: of Late-Quaternary Environments of the United States*, 53–71. Minneapolis: University of Minnesota Press, 1983.

Ward, H. A. "The Willamette Meteorite." *Proceedings of the Rochester Academy of Science* 4 (March 1904): 137–48.

Ward, H. A. "The Willamette Meteorite." *Scientific American Supplement* 58 (July 9, 1904): 23838–40.

Watson, Bruce McIntyre. *Lives Lived West of the Divide: A Biographical Dictionary of Fur Traders Working West of the Rockies, 1793-1858*. 3 vols. Kelowna: University of British Columbia, Okanagan, 2010.

Weaver, Charles E. *The Mineral Resources of Stevens County*. Washington Geological Survey Bulletin no. 20. Olympia, WA: Frank M. Lamborn, 1920.

Webster, John M. Papers. Manuscripts, Archives, and Special Collections, Washington State University Libraries, Pullman.

Wells, Martin J. *Tramway Titan: Byron Riblet, Wire Rope, and Western Resource Towns*. Victoria, BC: Trafford Publishing, 2005.

Wehr, Wesley. *The Accidental Collector: Art, Fossils, and Friendships*. Seattle: University of Washington Press, 2004.

Wehr, W. C. "Eocene Fossil Plants of the Okanogan Highlands." *Douglasia* (Winter 1984): 13–14.

Wehr, W. C., and D. Q. Hopkins. "The Eocene Orchards and Gardens of Republic, Washington." *Washington Geology* 22, no. 3 (Sept. 1994), 27–34.

Wehr, Wesley. *The Eighth Lively Art: Conversations with Painters, Poets, Musicians, and the Wicked Witch of the West*. Seattle: University of Washington Press, 2001.

Wehr, Wesley C. and Steven R. Manchester. "Paleobotanical Significance of Ecene Flowers, Fruits, and Seeds from Republic, Washington." *Washington Geology* 24, no. 2 (June 1996), 25–27.

Winchell, N. H. "Another Meteorite in the Supreme Court." *American Geologist* 36 (1905): 247–49.

Winchell, N. H. "The Willamette Meteorite." *American Geologist* 36 (1905): 250–57.

Wolfe, J. A., and W. Wehr. *Middle Eocene Dicotyledonous Plants from Republic, Northeastern Washington*. U.S. Geological Survey Bulletin 1597. 1987.

Zenk, Henry, and Tony Johnson. *Chinuk Wawa as Our Elders Teach Us to Speak It*. Confederated Tribes of the Grande Ronde, 2012.

INDEX

L

ABOUT THE AUTHOR

Spokane-based teacher and naturalist JACK NISBET is the author of several books that explore the human and natural history of the intermountain West, including *Purple Flat Top*, *Singing Grass Burning Sage*, and *Visible Bones*. He has also written two books that trace fur agent and cartographer David Thompson's travels west of the Continental Divide: *Sources of the River* and *The Mapmaker's Eye*.

Nisbet's recent focus on the naturalist David Douglas resulted in his biography *The Collector*, which was named a Pacific Northwest Booksellers Association 2010 Book of the Year. *David Douglas: A Naturalist at Work*, published in 2012, is an illustrated collection of essays that aims to connect Douglas's vision of the Northwest landscape to what we see today. It also served as the companion to a museum exhibit about Douglas, curated by Nisbet and his wife, Claire.